Bed and Sofa

KINOfiles Film Companions

General Editor: Richard Taylor

Written for cineastes and students alike, KINOfiles are readable, authoritative, illustrated companion handbooks to the most important and interesting films to emerge from Russian cinema from its beginnings to the present. Each KINOfile investigates the production, context and reception of the film and the people who made it, and analyses the film itself and its place in Russian and World cinema. KINOfiles also include films of the other countries that once formed part of the Soviet Union, as well as works by émigré filmmakers working in the Russian tradition.

KINOfiles form a part of KINO: The Russian Cinema Series.

BED AND SOFA:
The Film Companion

JULIAN GRAFFY

KINOfile Film Companion 5

I.B.Tauris *Publishers*
LONDON • NEW YORK

Published in 2001 by I.B.Tauris & Co Ltd,
6 Salem Road, London W2 4BU
175 Fifth Avenue, New York NY 10010
www.ibtauris.com

In the United States of America and in Canada distributed by
St. Martin's Press, 175 Fifth Avenue, New York NY 10010

ISBN 1 86064 503 8

A full CIP record for this book is available from the British Library
A full CIP record for this book is available from the Library of Congress

Library of Congress catalog card: available

Typeset in Monotype Calisto by Ewan Smith, London
Printed and bound in Great Britain by MPG Books Ltd, Bodmin

Contents

Illustrations

Nos 1, 2, 10, 13, Muzei kino, Moscow; nos 3, 4, 6–8, 11, 12, 14, BFI Films: Stills, posters and designs; nos 5, 9, courtesy of Richard Taylor.

Acknowledgements

I wish to thank Richard Taylor both for inviting me to contribute this volume to the I.B.Tauris *KINOfile* series, and for his consistent encouragement and patience while I was at work on it.

I am profoundly grateful to Josephine Woll, both for reading the typescript with sympathetic attention and perspicacity, and for a number of valuable suggestions.

Birgit Beumers, James Mann, Milena Michalski, Andrei Rogatchevski, Natasha Synessios, Richard Taylor and Evgeni Tsymbal all helped me greatly by supplying me with materials used in this study. I am very grateful to them.

I owe, as ever, a huge debt of gratitude to the energy, good humour and resourcefulness of the staff of the Library of the School of Slavonic and East European Studies, University College London.

Production Credits

English title: **BED AND SOFA**
Original Russian title: **TRET'IA MESHCHANSKAIA** [Third
                                       Meshchanskaia Street]
Alternative Russian title: **LIUBOV' VTROEM** [Three in Love,
                                       Ménage à trois]

Production company: Sovkino, Moscow, 1927
Release date: 15 March 1927
Theme and libretto: Viktor Shklovsky
Director: Abram Room
Screenplay: Viktor Shklovsky, Abram Room
Assistants: Sergei Iutkevich, E. Kuzis
Director of photography: Grigori Giber
Design: Vasili Rakhals, Sergei Iutkevich
Length: 68 minutes, 2025 metres

Cast

Kolia [Nikolai], the husband	Nikolai Batalov
Liuda [Liudmila], the wife	Liudmila Semenova
Volodia [Vladimir], the friend	Vladimir Fogel
The yardman	Leonid Iurenev
The nurse	Maria Iarotskaia

Bed and Sofa is available on video in the USA from International
Historic Films

Note on Transliteration and Dates

The transliteration system used for proper names in the text of this study is that of the Library of Congress, without diacritics, with the following emendations: (a) when a Russian name has a clear English version, such as Eisenstein, Mayakovsky, that is preferred; (b) when a Russian surname ends in -ii or -yi, this is replaced by a single -y, e.g. Shklovsky; (c) when a Russian given name ends in -ii, this is replaced by a single i, e.g. Grigori.

The standard Library of Congress system is used in the Notes and the Further Reading.

When he gets up in the morning at the beginning of the film, Kolia tears a page from a tear-off calendar on which we can clearly see the number 3, though the day of the week below it is not clear, and there is no reference to the year. Later he announces to his wife, Liudmila: 'Today is Saturday – don't forget to clean the floors.' These references to time are followed by three specific temporal references in succeeding intertitles. The first says that 'Fogel had already lived at the Batalovs' for three days'. The next, 'The morning of 9 July', is the day Kolia leaves Moscow on business. This is followed by a title '14 July, The Aviation and Chemical Society Day'. The sketch of the set design by Sergei Iutkevich also clearly shows a calendar with the year 1926.

All this evidence clearly dates the events of the film to the summer of 1926, the year the film was made, in which 3 July was indeed a Saturday, as confirmed by D. Crystal (ed.), *The Cambridge Factfinder*, 3rd edn (Cambridge, 1998) p. 148. A later intertitle takes the film's story on into the autumn.

When Kolia returns from his business trip, he sees that the calendar has not been touched in his absence. At this point a close-up of the calendar clearly shows both the date, the 9th, and the day, Saturday. But, obviously, the 3rd and the 9th cannot be the same day of the week – if 3 July was a Saturday, then the 9th would be a Friday. The explanation would seem to be that in October 1926, when, as the cameraman Grigori Giber reports, the film's interiors were being shot, the tear-off calendar's pages for July had long been consigned to the rubbish bin. The crew simply used the pages for the current month, trusting in the fact that the month itself was not indicated; 9 October 1926 was, indeed, a Saturday.

Some commentators have set the film in 1927, when 9 July *was* a Saturday, though this in turn raises the problem that 3 July 1927 was a Sunday, which goes contrary to Kolia's initial statement. They have used their conjecture to suggest that the film makes direct reference to the political developments of July 1927, but, since shooting was completed at the end of 1926 and the film premiered in March 1927, this possibility can be excluded.

1. Introduction: Before *Bed and Sofa*

Abram Matveevich Room, the director of *Bed and Sofa*, was born on 16 June 1894 (old style) in the town of Vilno (now Vilnius, the capital of independent Lithuania, but then part of the Russian Empire). In 1914 he entered the Neuropsychological Institute in Petrograd where he studied medicine. His famous cinematic contemporary, Dziga Vertov, two years Room's junior, made a similar journey, from the provincial town of Białystok (now in Poland), entering the Institute in 1916. In 1917 Room moved to Saratov, where he continued his studies in the medical faculty of the university. During the Civil War, in 1918, he was sent by the Red Army to work as a doctor on the Volga.

Room had been interested in the theatre since childhood, and he participated in the nationalisation of the art institutions in Saratov in 1918. In 1920 he became the director of the Saratov Young People's Theatre, staging plays and running theatre workshops. In 1923 the People's Commissar for Enlightenment, Anatoli Lunacharsky, visited the town. He invited Room to Moscow and introduced him to Vsevolod Meyerhold. Room began work at the Theatre of the Revolution, which Meyerhold headed, directing Aleksei Faiko's play *Lake Liul*, the story of a petit-bourgeois intellectual's coming to revolutionary consciousness. The play premiered on 8 November 1923, for the sixth anniversary of the Revolution, and was widely discussed in the

Soviet press. Room recalls that even at this stage his interest in the cinema was growing and that it influenced his staging of the play. Soon afterwards he met Esfir Shub, later one of the leading Soviet documentary film-makers but then working as an editor at the exhibition section of Goskino, the State Cinema Organisation, and under her influence he himself made the move to cinema.[1]

The First State Film Factory [Pervaia Goskinofabrika] had been established in 1923 in the former Khanzhonkov Studios on Zhitnaia Street in Moscow in 1923.[2] Room began work there the following year, as an assistant to the director Czesław Sabiński. The first film he directed himself was called *Guess What MOS Says* [Chto govorit 'MOS', sei otgadaite vopros, 1924], an advertisement reel for the Moscow Advertisement Bureau, which, with its eccentric tricks, Room turned into a calling card for his own work. It was followed by *The Chase for Home-Brew* [Gonka za samogonkoi, 1924] a propaganda film against alcoholism, which Goskino considered to be too naturalistic and negative, instructing that Room should be given no further films to direct and should be sacked from the studio.[3] But the studio managed to keep him on and in 1925 he directed his first full-length film *The Bay of Death* [Bukhta smerti]. Set during the Civil War in a southern port held by the Whites, it tells the story of a middle-aged mechanic who comes to realise the rightness of the Red cause. Even in this ideologically charged tale, Room shows both an acute concern with the fate of the individual and an interest in the role of objects and setting. It was followed in 1926 by *The Traitor* [Predatel'], set in the pre-Revolutionary period, in which a tsarist agent provokes a group of revolutionary soldiers to a doomed rebellion, which is mercilessly crushed. After the Revolution the provocateur is exposed by the Cheka and punished.[4]

During this period Room also played a leading role in ARK, the Association of Revolutionary Cinematography [Assotsiatsiia revoliutsionnoi kinematografii] which had been set up in February 1924 as an action group to encourage government interest in the cinema, and to make sure that the films that were made had an ideologically correct stance. He was a member of the ARK board, a leader of their Thursday meetings which discussed new films and cinematic issues of importance, and a member of the board of the association's journal, *Kinozhurnal ARK* (renamed *Kinofront* in 1926), to which he

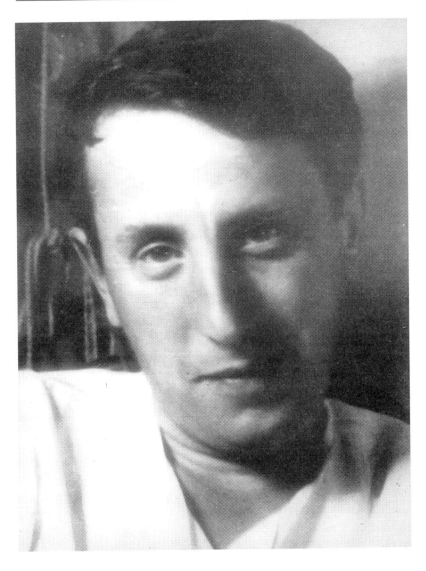

1. Portrait of Abram Room, 1920s

contributed a number of articles.[5] Such was Room's fame in the
1920s that he was linked with Eisenstein and Kuleshov, Pudovkin
and Vertov as one of the 'big five' directors in Soviet cinema.

Room wrote the screenplay of *Bed and Sofa* in collaboration with

Viktor Shklovsky (1893–1984), one of the leading members of the Formalist group of literary theorists and a close associate of Mayakovsky and other Futurist poets. Like the other major Formalist critics, Boris Eikhenbaum and Iuri Tynianov, Shklovsky was very influential in the Soviet cinema as a critic and theoretician, but also through direct involvement as the scriptwriter of films in a variety of genres ranging from literary adaptations to adventure stories, from revolutionary material to tales of everyday life. He wrote the intertitles for *The Bay of Death* and worked on the script of *The Traitor*. He adapted Jack London's 1907 story 'The Unexpected' for Lev Kuleshov's *By the Law* [Po zakonu, also known as Dura Lex, 1926]. He also worked on two other films about the experience of women in the Moscow of NEP, the New Economic Policy introduced by the Bolshevik government in March 1921 with the purpose of restoring the economy by allowing some private enterprise. He wrote the intertitles for Oleg Frelikh's social drama *Prostitute* [Prostitutka, 1926], and contributed to the script of Boris Barnet's social comedy *The House on Trubnaia* [Dom na Trubnoi, 1927]. In lectures on writing for the screen delivered in the late 1920s he insisted that 'the classic screenplay has a small number of actors, simple relations between them, with each story completed, so that there are no unresolved fates, and with precise, small episodes', words that make the open ending of *Bed and Sofa* all the more striking.[6]

The film's cameraman, Grigori Giber (1891–1951) had begun working in the cinema in 1907. During the Civil War he served as a photographer at the front and took part in the work of the agit-train *The October Revolution*. After the Revolution he made newsreels, including newsreels of Lenin, and educational films. The designer, Vasili Rakhals (1890–1942) had started out in the theatre, and began to work in films in 1915. By the time of *Bed and Sofa* he had already worked on Room's *The Bay of Death* and *The Traitor*, Sergei Eisenstein's *Strike* [Stachka, 1925] and *The Battleship Potemkin* [Bronenosets Potemkin, 1925], and Lev Kuleshov's *The Death Ray* [Luch smerti, 1925], all of them made at the First Film Factory.[7] He was assisted by Sergei Iutkevich (1904–85), who in 1922, along with Grigori Kozintsev, Leonid Trauberg and Georgi Kryzhitsky, had written the notorious *Eccentric Manifesto* of the young group of theatrical and cinema directors known as FEKS [Factory of the Eccentric Actor].

After work with various theatrical groups, he co-directed with S. Griunberg the short film *You Give Us Radio!* [Daesh' radio!, 1925] an eccentric comedy set among the Moscow homeless. Moving to the First Film Factory, he was an assistant to Room on *The Traitor*.

The actors whom Room chose to play the three central roles in *Bed and Sofa* came to the film from very different backgrounds. Nikolai Batalov (1899–1937) was born in Moscow and had worked at the Moscow Arts Theatre since 1916. He openly acknowledged the influence of Konstantin Stanislavsky on his acting style. In the early 1920s, like all the leading Arts Theatre actors, he was 'afraid of the cinema' which he considered 'something which you should not take up seriously. It was shameful and ignominious.'[8] He was eventually persuaded to play the small part of the Red Army soldier Gusev in Iakov Protazanov's *Aelita* [1924] and he followed this up with the part of another young man of exemplary political credentials, Pavel Vlasov, the hero of Pudovkin's *The Mother* [Mat´, 1926], taken from Maxim Gorky's epic story of the revolutionary struggle.

Liudmila Semenova (1899–1990) was born in St Petersburg where her father was a maths teacher and her mother an opera singer. She studied at the Tvorchestvo Film Studio, run in Moscow by Boris Chaikovsky, for nine months, starting in the autumn of 1918, while at the same time working as a nurse in an evacuation hospital. She played a number of small roles in films as part of her studies, but when she graduated in the summer of 1919 she found parts hard to come by, since in her own words her looks did not suit her for the films being made by the new nationalised cinema. She studied dance in 1921 and worked in Nikolai Foregger's Mastfor theatre in Moscow from 1921 to 1924. In 1924–25 she was an actress at the Svobodnyi teatr [Free Theatre] in Leningrad and worked as a dancer and singer in operetta. Her first major film role was that of Valia in *The Devil's Wheel* [Chertovo koleso, 1926], directed by Kozintsev and Trauberg, a part which required her to cut and dye her hair, and in which she discovered the look she retains in *Bed and Sofa*. Valia is a girl drawn to the excitements and the bright lights of NEP, who temporarily drags the film's hero Vania, a sailor from the *Avrora*, the ship that started the Revolution, down with her into the criminal underworld. The film prefigures *Bed and Sofa* in that its hero is a member of the armed forces torn between solidarity with his comrades and the

2. The cast and crew of *Bed and Sofa*. Room is in the middle of the back row; Fogel, Semenova and Batalov are in the front row, on the right

charms of an attractive woman. Unlike *Bed and Sofa*, however, its sympathies are entirely with the man, who turns out to be susceptible to the call of duty and the Revolution, and goes back to his ship. Valia, on the other hand, is too weak to pull herself out of the mire, but her ultimate fate is of no concern to the film-makers and she is simply erased from the film.

In her memoirs of working on *Bed and Sofa*, Semenova recalls having seen Batalov at the Moscow Arts Theatre in 1916 and the trepidation she felt at the prospect of working with him.[9] She had already acted with the third member of the film's triangle, Vladimir Fogel, at Foregger's theatre. Fogel (1902–29) was born in Moscow to a family of Russified Germans. He studied at the Technological Institute and then at Kuleshov's Workshop, where he did all his own stunts and soon gained a reputation as one of the most talented and versatile of Kuleshov's actors. He had a small part in Kuleshov's *The Extraordinary Adventures of Mr West in the Land of the Bolsheviks* [Neobychainye prikliucheniia Mistera Vesta v strane bol'shevikov, 1924], played Fog, a fascist, in his *The Death Ray*, and the murderer, Michael Dennin, in his *By the Law*. He played in Otsep and Barnet's *Miss Mend* [1926] and in Protazanov's comedy *The Three Millions Trial* [Protsess o trekh millionakh, 1926]. He played the starring role of the young man obsessed by chess in the short *Chess Fever* [Shakhmatnaia goriachka], which Pudovkin and Nikolai Shpikovsky directed in 1925. Such, indeed, was the range of his roles, that critics nicknamed him 'the one-man orchestra'.[10]

This small band of people, all of them born between 1890 and 1904, and thus themselves the contemporaries of the cinema, came together in the summer of 1926 to make one of the finest of Soviet silent films, and one that gives perhaps the most vivid picture of the life of the period, *Bed and Sofa*.

Notes

1. On Room's early life see especially his 1968 autobiography in V. Zabrodin (ed.), *Abram Matveevich Room. 1894–1976. Materialy k retrospektive fil'mov* (Moscow, 1994), pp. 7–8; V. B. Shklovskii, *Room. Zhizn' i rabota* (Moscow, 1929); reprinted in his *Za 60 let. Raboty o kino* (Moscow, 1985), pp. 135–9; and I. Grashchenkova, *Abram Room* (Moscow, 1977), pp. 231–44.

2. Goskino was renamed Sovkino in 1924, but the studio retained the title First State Film Factory until 1926. *Bed and Sofa* is thus the first of Room's films made at the studio to bear the credit Sovkino (Moscow).

3. On Room's early work at the studio, see his memoir, 'Iunost' byvaet odnazhdy. Vspominaet Abram Room', *Iskusstvo kino*, 2, 1974, pp. 14–16; and a memoir by Mikhail Kapchinskii, Head of the First Film Factory in 1925–26, 'Na ulitse Zhitnoi', in *Zhizn' v kino. Veterany o sebe i svoikh tovarishchakh*, Vol. 2 (Moscow, 1979), pp. 56–74 (pp. 58–61).

4. On *The Bay of Death* see especially Grashchenkova, *Abram Room*, pp. 19–32; on *The Traitor*, see ibid., pp. 32–5.

5. On ARK see R. Taylor and I. Christie (eds), *The Film Factory: Russian and Soviet Cinema in Documents 1896–1939* (London, 1988), p. 101, and see its 'Declaration', first published in *Pravda*, 27 February 1924, in ibid., p. 103.

6. Quoted from *Istoriia sovetskogo kino*, Vol. 1 (Moscow, 1969), p. 475.

7. On Giber see S. I. Iutkevich (ed.), *Kinoslovar'* (Moscow, 1986), pp. 95–6 and Grashchenkova, *Abram Room*, p. 87; on Rakhal's, see *Kinoslovar'*, p. 344.

8. N. P. Batalov, [Moia rabota v kino], in *Nikolai Petrovich Batalov. Stat'i,*

vospominaniia, pis'ma (Moscow, 1971), pp. 32–7 (p. 32). On Batalov see also M. Tsikounas, *Les origines du cinéma soviétique. Un regard neuf* (Paris, 1992), pp. 104–7; and V. Turitsyn, 'Nikolai Batalov', *Aktery sovetskogo kino*, Vol. 2 (Moscow, 1966), pp. 31–42.

9. Semenova has written two memoirs of working on *Bed and Sofa*: 'Zhizn' snachala', in *Zhizn' v kino. Veterany o sebe i svoikh tovarishchakh*, Vol. 1 (Moscow, 1971), pp. 312–27; and an untitled memoir of Batalov in *Nikolai Petrovich Batalov. Stat'i, vospominaniia, pis'ma*, pp. 163–5.

10. Quoted from Tsikounas, *Les origines du cinéma soviétique*, p. 112. On Fogel', see E. Arnol'di, 'Vladimir Fogel'', *Aktery sovetskogo kino*, Vol. 4 (Moscow, 1968), pp. 232–43; E. Lyndina, 'Polet komety', *Ekran*, 1, 1995, pp. 40–1; and Tsikounas, pp. 112–15.

2. *Bed and Sofa*: An Analysis

Plot Synopsis

Early one July morning in 1926 Volodia, a young print worker, speeds into Moscow by train in search of work. Moscow itself is still asleep and so are the inhabitants of a flat on Third Meshchanskaia Street: Kolia, a foreman on a construction site, and his wife Liuda.

As the train arrives, Kolia and Liuda get up and Kolia leaves for his work rebuilding the Bolshoi Theatre. Volodia wanders around Moscow and soon gets himself a job, but because of the housing shortage finds it impossible to arrange a place to live.

Liuda is preparing dinner when suddenly Volodia bursts into the flat, accompanied by Kolia. It turns out that they had served together in the Red Army, and that, meeting Volodia in the street, Kolia has invited him to sleep on their sofa. Three days pass and Volodia is registered as an inhabitant of the flat but without the right to further living space.

On the morning of 9 July Volodia returns from work with gifts of a radio and a copy of the magazine *Novyi mir* [New Life]. Kolia receives a telegram instructing him to go on a work trip. Volodia, in embarrassment, proposes moving out for the duration of the trip, but Kolia insists that he stay.

On 14 July Volodia takes Liuda to the celebrations for the annual festival of the Society of the Friends of Aviation and Chemical Construction. They take a flight high over Moscow and then visit the cinema. On their return to the flat they begin an affair, and a hand-shake seals Volodia's move from the sofa to the bed.

On 18 July Kolia returns from his trip, and during dinner Volodia confesses to the affair and offers to move out. Instead Kolia leaves, but he too can find nowhere else to stay and attempts to sleep on an office desk.

When, one rainy day, Kolia returns bedraggled to the flat for his things, Liuda takes pity on him and offers him the sofa. So they are a trio again, and the men soon settle to a regular evening game of draughts, leaving Liuda restless and bored. Gradually, however, tensions grow between them, and Volodia, jealous that Liuda may be waiting for Kolia's return from work, locks the flat door and, pocket-ing the key, returns to sleep on the sofa. That night Kolia is forced to get in through the window and sleep on the rocking chair. Waking, Liuda takes pity on him and he ends up back in the bed.

Two months pass. Liuda has a fainting fit while doing the washing, and Volodia announces to Kolia that she is pregnant. The men, neither of whom is certain who is the father, insist that she have an abortion.

Liuda goes to a private abortion clinic, where a number of women are waiting, but when her turn eventually comes she changes her mind and leaves. She returns to the flat on Third Meshchanskaia Street, packs up and leaves a note for the two men, informing them that she will never return. As Liuda makes her way to the railway station the two men arrive together at the clinic. Informed of the new turn of events they return to the flat and read her farewell note. After an initial admission of their reprehensible behaviour, they settle down to tea and jam. The film ends with Liuda at the train window, speeding away from Moscow.

Room's Plans for the Film

In an article entitled 'Cinema and Theatre', published on 19 May 1925 in the journal *Sovetskii ekran* [Soviet Screen], Room had insisted that 'Cinema is pre-eminently realism, life, the everyday, objectivity, properly motivated behaviour, rational gesture', adding that *'theatre is "seeming" whereas cinema is "being"'*.[1] The same aesthetic informs a statement of intent he gave to the film magazine *Kino* before embarking upon *Bed and Sofa*. Room's words are so revealing about his intentions and methods, that the statement is given in full here:[2]

> After several pictures conceived on the grand scale and weighed down by the large number of characters, there is now an urgent need to work on a film in which all the material is not dispersed and fragmented, but compressed, condensed and concentrated, and where we stake everything on the acting,[3] and on maximising the inventiveness of the scriptwriter, the director and the cameraman.[4]
>
> The slogan of a picture of this kind is – aesthetic economy.
>
> It is not just Italian book-keeping which must be in the forefront of the struggle for a regime of economy, but also the book-keeping of creative work, which must decisively embark upon artistic staff reductions.[5]
>
> The material is condensed and packed into a small expanse of time, a single room and Moscow exteriors. The three characters in the picture set off lightly with this baggage on their film journey.
>
> The journey lasts eight reels, during which all the sparingly applied movements, the gestures, the camera angles, the objects, should be used, transposed and played with in such a way that they can live in the viewer's consciousness not only before but also after the end of the film.
>
> The setting is familiar to each and everyone – a Moscow flat, or more precisely '33 square arshins of living space',[6] which belongs to an ordinary Soviet employee and is situated in a semi-basement, from the only window of which you can see a reflection of the life of the town. But in fact you can only see half of it; the semi-basement window, like a curtain pulled down over the street, lets you see only the hurrying legs of the passers-by, car tyres and the hoofs of the coachmen's nags.
>
> This room on the real Third Meshchanskaia Street, which is near the Sukharev Tower,[7] is populated by things. Each of them has its fate, its past, present and future. Together they all live, breathe, interfere in people's lives and keep them in close captivity.
>
> Love, marriage, the family and sexual morality are pressing contemporary topics, which have been discussed thoroughly in the press and at public debates and have found a partial reflection even on the theatrical stage, but have not yet been touched upon at all by the

cinema. Or more precisely, the Soviet cinema has not yet tackled them in earnest, and if it has come upon them by chance, it has shown a shallow, primitive 'delicacy'. We were hypocrites, some rules of decency (which were not registered anywhere) stopped us if not resolving then at least sharpening, revealing and posing these subjects for discussion by cinema audiences in a serious and real way (maybe even in a sharp and coarse way).

That intimate 'honour' and that well-groomed chastity with which the relations between men and women have been approached in films must be exposed once and for all. We have fed the viewer with sweet fairy-tales about nimble storks and magic cabbage patches for long enough!

We must start to use real words where so far all we have heard is giggling and lisping.

The content of the picture in short: two men live with one woman. The triangle which has never closed up before – the husband, the wife, the lover – closes up and takes shape officially. The woman does not conceal the second man from the first and formalises this life as a trio. But for several reasons their life as a threesome collapses. A long sequence of tragic and tragicomic interconnections tangles their life up and the woman, who had been the most passive component in this complex equation, ruptures it by her departure. The wife is played by Liudmila Semenova (who played Valia in *The Devil's Wheel*), the husband, who is a foreman on the site where the Lenin Institute is being built,[8] by Nikolai Batalov (who played in *Aelita* and *The Mother*), and the technician in the printing works by Vladimir Fogel (who was in *The Death Ray*, *Miss Mend* and *By the Law*).

In formal terms we shall apply several new devices.

The film camera, which so far has been just an impassive observer of events, goes into the very thick of the action, looks at the world through the eyes of the heroes and lives alongside them. In the structure of the frame and in the editing we shall use the device of shot–counter-shot, which will sharpen the picture's dynamism. The script was written by Viktor Shklovsky. The crew consists of the camera operator Grigori Giber, the assistant and designer Sergei Iutkevich, the assistant E. Kuzis, the set designer Vasili Rakhals and the production manager A. Kotosheva.

We plan to complete filming in two and a half months.

The picture will use Moscow exteriors: the building sites of the Central Telegraph and the Lenin Institute, outdoor celebrations at the Agricultural Exhibition, the annual festival of the Society of the Friends of Aviation and Chemical Construction and various shots of morning and evening Moscow.

Thus Room alerts the reader both to the concerns of his new film and to his cinematic method. His two previous pictures had both been on historical subjects, and the ideologically safe historical-revolutionary theme had been widely addressed in recent years, notably in the films of Eisenstein and Pudovkin.

Though contemporary life had not been ignored by the Soviet cinema, frankness in the treatment of this subject matter, and particularly of sexual mores, presented obvious problems. As Room suggests, sexual morality was widely discussed in the press, with Party surveys of sexual behaviour being regularly printed, especially in the Young Communist League newspaper *Komsomol'skaia pravda*, and public lectures and debates on the subject were extremely popular. Writing in 1926 about the popularity of these lectures, a Komsomol journalist called talk about sex the 'hit' [boevik] of the season: 'every speaker must have "the problem of sex" in his repertoire; all other questions of social life are perceived as supplementary material that must inevitably be listened to along with the "hit".'[9] But, as Eric Naiman notes, following Michel Foucault, 'An encouraged discourse [...] may be a more effective form of control than censorship', leading him to conclude that, 'By 1927 the sexual question was a constant topic of nondebate', and to describe the discussion of sex during NEP as part of 'the collective manipulation of young Soviet men and women'.[10]

Room goes on to insist that the cinema has been especially circumspect in the treatment of these issues, a point of view borne out by the observations of Walter Benjamin, who lived in Moscow from 6 December 1926 until the end of January 1927 (which was the time when *Bed and Sofa* was being edited), and noted in his diary:

A serious critique of Soviet man is impossible in film, which is not the case with theater. But the representation of bourgeois life is likewise impossible [...] Above all, however, Russian film knows nothing of eroticism. As is well known, the 'bagatellization' of love and sex life is part and parcel of the communist credo. It would be considered counterrevolutionary propaganda to represent tragic love entanglements on film or stage. There remains the possibility of social comedy whose satirical target would essentially be the new bourgeoisie. Whether film, one of the most advanced machines for the imperialist domination of the masses, can be expropriated on this basis, that is very much the question.[11]

If it is Room's stated intention to address questions of sexual morality with a new frankness, it is explicitly not his intention to provide a final answer, but rather to pose 'these subjects for discussion by cinema audiences in a serious and real way'. A key to his approach must be sought in the phrase 'We have fed the viewer with sweet fairy-tales [...] for long enough', which makes a direct allusion to the famous sentence in the introduction to Mikhail Lermontov's 1840 novel *A Hero of Our Times* in which the narrator expresses his philosophy: stating that, 'We have fed people with sweets for long enough', he goes on to suggest that he is happy merely to 'draw contemporary man as he understands him, and, to his and your misfortune, has too often met him. It will be sufficient that the sickness is pointed out, but as for how to cure it, God knows!'[12] Like Lermontov before him, Room intends to offer a portrait of 'heroes' of his time, to show people as they really are, but not to dictate the viewer's assessment of their behaviour. His approach was amply rewarded by the widespread discussion provoked by the film, but its open ending would trouble many viewers, both on its Soviet release and for years to come.

The Film-making Process

The First Film Factory attracted a number of leading writers and critics as scriptwriters, including Isaak Babel, Sergei Tretiakov and Viktor Shklovsky. Room recalls that Shklovsky approached him in the canteen with an idea based upon a tale of the new sexual mores he had read in *Komsomolskaia pravda*. Two young men had turned up together at a maternity hospital where a woman had given birth to a son, both claiming to be the father of the child, since the young woman considered herself the wife of both of them and did not know which was the father. All three were members of the Komsomol and of the Workers' Educational Faculty [rabfakovtsy]. They called their relationship a *ménage à trois* and insisted that as Komsomol members they were immune to feelings of jealousy.[13] Shklovsky and Room worked on the script in July 1926 in the Crimea, where, along with Mayakovsky and Lili Brik, they were filming the documentary *Jews on the Land* [Evrei na zemle] about an attempt to establish a Jewish agricultural settlement. They finished it on the train on the way back to Moscow. During the process of refining the script they gradually removed various tendentious scenes, including one in which a commission from the House Committee comes to the flat and its chairman attacks the behaviour of the inhabitants.[14]

The cameraman, Grigori Giber, recalls that they started shooting exteriors very early on the morning of 23 August 1926, filming from a car, in the street, from the tops of the Lenin Institute and the Bolshoi Theatre. They even filmed on Third Meshchanskaia Street, the street in which the film was set, but the crowds were so great that they were forced to film at 3 a.m.[15] Sergei Iutkevich, also involved in the filming of the street scenes, described Moscow itself, in a contemporary report, as a 'fantastic stage set' [fantasticheskaia dekoratsiia].[16] *Bed and Sofa* was the first Soviet film to make such extensive use of Moscow exteriors, and the outdoor scenes that punctuate the film, along with its regular specific references to time, gave the contemporary viewer an unprecedented sense that this story was unfolding in a recognisable world, observed with almost documentary precision. As Room later recalled, 'I wanted the film shot in long sequences: I began to like long extracts of life', adding that he wanted the viewer to watch the film 'not on a bicycle but on foot'.[17]

At the end of September they moved into the studio where they worked for a further thirty-five days.[18] Sergei Iutkevich, the set designer, reports that he built a set with four walls, any one of which could be removed so that filming could take place from any angle, but Semenova recalls that when Room and Giber saw the 'neat 5 x 5 metre cube' Giber could not imagine where he would be able to put his lights and Room exclaimed 'Is that a set?! […] It's a box!!' Workmen had to be employed to drag the walls apart.[19] The set was given all facilities, even a real water supply and toilet, and people working on the film hung their coats in the cupboard and cooked their lunch on the primus stove. When a cat took up residence with

3. Set design by Sergei Iutkevich

its kittens, Giber even shot some scenes from the cat's point of view by crawling around on his stomach with a wind-up camera, shots which, to his regret, were removed from the final cut. According to Room, the actors felt so at home on the set that sometimes they spent the night there.[20] It was Room's practice first to talk through the episodes thoroughly with the actors and discuss their moves, and then to shoot no more than three takes, since he was eager that they should not 'overplay' their scenes and also concerned about the shortage of film stock. He was very ready to listen to suggestions, and took up several ideas proposed by Batalov and Fogel.[21]

The Film's Titles

Liubov′ vtroem / Three in Love / Ménage à trois
The film's original title was *Liubov′ vtroem* (literally, 'triple love'), the Russian term for a love triangle or *ménage à trois*. Considered too bold

and scandalous, it was replaced by *Tret'ia Meshchanskaia* [Third Meshchanskaia Street], by which the film is now known in Russia, but in fact *Liubov' vtroem* was restored for the advertising posters,[22] and used in distribution. Contemporary reviews of the film use the two titles interchangeably (a practice not unusual at the time).

For most of the century before the making of *Bed and Sofa*, Russian culture had been preoccupied with the elaboration of new social models. One of the most persistently alluring of these was the idealised *ménage à trois*, which found its most notorious expression in Nikolai Chernyshevsky's 1863 novel *What is to be Done?* [Chto delat'?], subtitled 'From Tales About New People' [Iz rasskazov o novykh liudiakh]. It was drawn in part from literary models, including the writings of George Sand and Rousseau, and in part from the living arrangements of two famous contemporaries, Alexander Herzen and Nikolai Shelgunov. Herzen, who had himself addressed the question of the love triangle in his 1847 novel *Who is to Blame?* [Kto vinovat?], participated in two such triangles, first with his wife Natalie and the German Romantic poet Georg Herwegh, and then with his closest friend Nikolai Ogarev and Ogarev's second wife, Natalia Tuchkova-Ogareva. Despite the elevated belief of the participants that a continuing harmonious union was possible, both of these triangles ended in bitterness and recrimination. A more rational approach was taken by the radical critic Nikolai Shelgunov, his wife and cousin Liudmila Michaelis and the poet and political activist Mikhail Mikhailov, and this triple union for a time successfully combined political activity and personal tranquillity. After the arrest and death of Mikhailov, Michaelis spent a period in European exile, but she eventually returned to her husband.[23]

In *What is to be Done?*, Dmitri Lopukhov and Alexander Kirsanov are fellow medical students and already the greatest of friends before they meet the heroine, Vera Pavlovna Rozalskaia, and Vera Pavlovna is initially jealous of their friendship. Lopukhov and Vera Pavlovna marry, but theirs is a relationship based upon Lopukhov's rational idealism and the marriage remains celibate. Kirsanov, realising the nature of his own feelings for Vera Pavlovna, withdraws from their lives. Eventually, though, it becomes impossible to ignore the intensity of the love between Vera Pavlovna and Kirsanov, and *What is to be Done?* becomes the story of Lopukhov's selfless accommodation to this love. While he does, at one stage, propose that all three of them live together, for 'economic' reasons, a point that is taken up later by the novel's exemplary radical hero Rakhmetov, who is against the idea of jealousy in a 'developed' person and insists to Vera Pavlovna that the trio could have lived calmly and moved into one apartment, the offer is stoutly rejected by Vera Pavlovna. Lopukhov sacrifices himself in the name of her greater love for Kirsanov, even faking his own suicide so that they can be married.[24] At the end of the novel Lopukhov, now resurrected as the 'Canadian' Charles Beaumont, himself marries again and the two couples take up residence in a kind of commune, with adjoining apartments and flexible arrangements for achieving privacy. The behaviour of the characters in *What is to be Done?* is motivated throughout by utopian ideals, virtuous delicacy and a concern for the feelings of others, and it is crucial to note that, despite its reputation, there is no period of *ménage à trois* in the novel. It is also important that the relations of the characters are not affected by pregnancy or the birth of offspring, since the Russian utopian tradition was hostile to children.[25] In the delicacy of its characters' behaviour, the absence of an actual *ménage à trois*, the general erasure of the physical and the specific elision of the complications of pregnancy, the novel's abstraction contrasts markedly with the sardonic realism of *Bed and Sofa*. Chernyshevsky did, however, in works written later during his Siberian exile, address the *ménage à trois* directly, notably in the tellingly titled drama *Forbidden to Others* [Drugim nel'zia, 1867–69]. The heroine of this work is engaged to a student, but in his absence she marries his close friend. When he returns, and the feelings between him and the heroine are seen to persist, the husband proposes the solution of the *ménage à trois*.[26]

Thus the radical thinkers of the mid-nineteenth century, to whom both the politicians and the artists of the post-revolutionary period would naturally turn, had raised questions of sexual morality and specifically had theorised about the *ménage à trois*. But Shklovsky and Room could also draw upon more recent models. During the first decade of the twentieth century the Symbolist poets Dmitri Merezhkovsky and Zinaida Gippius combined a celibate marriage very similar to that of Lopukhov and Vera Pavlovna with a *ménage à trois* with Dmitri Filosofov.[27] During the same decade the younger

Symbolist poets Alexander Blok and Andrei Bely, themselves linked over many years by an intense 'love-hatred', were both in love with Blok's wife Liubov Mendeleeva, and events reached a dramatic climax in March 1906 when Mendeleeva almost left her husband for Bely.[28]

After the Revolution the politician and sexual theorist Alexandra Kollontai addressed the idea of the 'love of three' in a famous 1923 article 'Make Way for the Winged Eros' ['Dorogu krylatomu erosu']. Stressing that love is not just biologically motivated but also socially articulated, she invokes the treatment of the love triangle by Herzen and Chernyshevsky as attempts to solve an emotional drama created by bourgeois capitalism. She insists that 'the key' to the problem of the duality of love is now 'in the hands of the proletariat', and suggests that the dilemma of one woman loving two men or one man loving two women can be resolved through the proletarian ideal of 'love-comradeship', which will destroy the exclusivity of the bourgeois marriage and place all the participants within the collective. In the 'accomplished Communist society, love, "winged Eros", will be transformed into something completely unfamiliar to us [...] People's feelings will become collective ones, and inequality between the sexes, as well as the dependence of woman on man, will disappear without a trace, lost in the memory of past centuries.'[29] The article has an obviously utopian tone, but 'Three Generations', a story Kollontai wrote at the same time, which traces the evolving sexual mores of a mother, a daughter and a granddaughter in the same family, is more circumspect. Olga Sergeevna Veselovskaia, who represents the middle generation, for a while maintains a simultaneous relationship with two men, but ends up estranged from both of them.[30]

The most famous real-life triangle of the period was that of the poet Vladimir Mayakovsky, Lili Brik and her husband, the Formalist critic Osip Brik, with whom he also had a close friendship based on their discussion of his poetry. This relationship was very much in the public domain, since his passionate love for Lili had been the main subject of Mayakovsky's lyric poetry for a decade.[31] The complex interaction between life, art and theory is particularly apparent in this instance, since both men were professed admirers of *What is to be Done?* As Lili later recalled of the poet: 'One of his favourite books was Chernyshevsky's *What is to be Done?* He kept going back to it. The life described in it echoes ours. Mayakovsky seemed to take advice from Chernyshevsky about his personal affairs, and find support in him. *What is to be Done?* was the last book he read before his death.'[32]

All the texts and relationships articulated here had entered the cultural consciousness and worked as subtexts for *Bed and Sofa*, none more so than the life of Mayakovsky and the Briks. Shklovsky was a colleague of Brik through the school of Russian Formalism, and the Formalist critics and the Futurist poets were connected through the Left Front of the Arts (LEF). Room, too, was a close acquaintance, and indeed, as recounted above, the script of *Bed and Sofa* was written while its authors were collaborating with Lili Brik and Mayakovsky on *Jews on the Land*. But, in addition to this, Mayakovsky was such a dominant figure in Soviet culture in the 1920s that his imagery served as a kind of cultural barometer of the period, and many of the images used in *Bed and Sofa* have their source in his poetry.

Tret´ia Meshchanskaia / Third Meshchanskaia Street and *meshchanstvo*

The title chosen to replace the 'scandalous' *Liubov´ vtroem* is the name of an actual Moscow street, one of four (First, Second, Third and Fourth Meshchanskaia Streets) which run north from the Inner Ring Road [Sadovoe koltso, Garden Ring], to the east of Tverskaia Street. The streets date from the late seventeenth century when, in 1671, Tsar Aleksei Mikhailovich resettled there the traders and craftsman (*meshchane*, from the Belorussian *mesta*, Polish *miasto*, meaning town) from the Belorussian towns he had won back from Poland. In the late 1920s, soon after the film's release, the streets were renamed First, Second, Third and Fourth Civic [Grazhdanskaia] Streets. In 1957, in honour of the Sixth International Festival of Young People and Students, which had been held in Moscow that year, the Moscow City Council gave First Meshchanskaia Street the name which it bears to this day, Peace Prospect [Prospekt mira]. Third Meshchanskaia Street is currently known as Shchepkin Street [Ulitsa Shchepkina], after Mikhail Shchepkin, the famous nineteenth-century actor who had lived on it.[33]

Though Third Meshchanskaia Street does appear twice in the film, in the early morning scene at the beginning in which a lamplighter puts out the streetlight, and an evening scene near the end when

Kolia goes out for bread and the lamplighter lights it again, its use as the film's title is based not on the setting in the street itself but on the acquired implications of the noun *meshchanstvo*, from which the adjective is derived.

Initially the word *meshchanstvo* was merely descriptive. It was first introduced into the Russian legal code in a manifesto of 17 March 1775, in which it indicated urban dwellers who were not registered in the merchant class [kupechestvo]. The term was made more inclusive by Catherine the Great, and gradually, during the nineteenth century, it lost its close connection with a specific social stratum and took on ever more pejorative associations in intellectual discourse. It began to imply vulgarity, philistinism and narrowness of vision, very similar to the use of the term *petit-bourgeois* in Western European languages.[34] It was used in this sense by Herzen in his 1862–63 essay collection 'Ends and Beginnings' [Kontsy i nachala], in which he describes the difficulty art has in dealing with it and predicts its inevitable victory, a line which was then quoted by Merezhkovsky to open his 1906 essay 'The Coming Vulgarian' [Griadushchii kham], which likewise attacked bourgeois values. Maxim Gorky's first play, which premiered in March 1902 and revealed the social and generational tensions in the home of a wealthy provincial merchant, bore the emblematic title *Meshchane* (the play has several titles in English but is usually known as *Philistines*).

After the Revolution, of course, both the class and the vices ascribed to it should have disappeared and, when it became clear that they had not, the term was ritually invoked, by both writers and social commentators, to indicate the perverse survival of a force which encouraged the continuation of the old ways, and thus to explain the gap between the ideal and reality. It is precisely in this sense that the term is used by Mayakovsky, who asserts in the poem 'About Rubbish' [O driani], written in 1920–21, that 'From behind the back of the Russian Soviet Federative Socialist Republic the muzzle of the *meshchanin* has emerged', only to go on to insist that he is referring not to a class but to '*meshchane* of all classes and estates indiscriminately'.[35] The connected words '*bourgeois*' [burzhuaznyi] and '*petit-bourgeois*' [melko-burzhuaznyi] were among those listed by A. M. Selishchev as having 'changed their meaning' in the post-Revolutionary decade, and taken on negative overtones.[36]

Anxiety about the survival of the *petit-bourgeois* mentality had been exacerbated by the introduction of NEP (the New Economic Policy) in March 1921, an explicit compromise with the old order that allowed some '*bourgeois*' groups an official existence.[37] But, in Sheila Fitzpatrick's words: 'that did not mean that other classes were safe from the siren song of the bourgeoisie. The Bolsheviks believed that their revolution had interfered with the society's natural progression to capitalism, and they were constantly on guard against a spontaneous reversion. "Bourgeois" and "petty-bourgeois" influences were everywhere. Persons of any social class were liable to succumb to them.'[38]

In 1925, Martyn Liadov, the Rector of the Sverdlov Communist University in Moscow, wrote:

> We have created new forms of ritual, we have shaken the laws of the old morality, but we have not yet killed the petty bourgeois sitting within each of us. In this respect the dead seize the living entirely. The petty bourgeois character in each of us still exists and makes itself known in our attitude toward the family, toward each other, in our sexual relations, and in every aspect of our personal life.[39]

In fact, both the phenomenon and concern about it survived throughout the Soviet period. Writing about the Stalin years, Vera Dunham insists that 'In the Soviet world, meshchanstvo appears at every rung of the social scale', where it is characterised by an obsession with possessions and by social apathy, since 'Meshchanstvo does not fret except about private matters'.[40] Indeed, *meshchanstvo* is still anathematised in the post-Soviet period, which explains why the street is among the few not to have reverted to its pre-revolutionary name.

As will be apparent, several of the characteristics that indicate *meshchanstvo* afflict the protagonists of *Bed and Sofa* and the term was widely used in contemporary discussion of the film.

Bed and Sofa

Thus, both of its original Russian titles encapsulate key concerns of Room's film, but when it was shown in the West it acquired new titles, *Bed and Sofa* in England and Germany, *Three in a Basement* [*Trois dans un sous-sol*] in France. The title *Ménage à trois* was clearly considered too scandalous (the film was shown in England only after censorship cuts), and the implications of *Third Meshchanskaia Street* would obviously be lost on Western audiences. *Bed and Sofa* is also an appropriate title, given the different functions of the two pieces of furniture in the film, but it has the significant disadvantage of drawing the viewer's attention to the contrasts in the roles and fates of the two men. Neither Russian title implies such a distinction. Indeed, the gradual revelation of how alike they are is fundamental to the film's meaning.

The Characters' Names

The characters are introduced on their first appearance by intertitles naming them as 'Vladimir Fogel, a printer', 'The husband (Nikolai Batalov)' and 'The wife (Liudmila Semenova)'. These are, of course, the names of the actors, and the characters gain no other names during the course of the film. We learn from an intertitle that 'Fogel had already lived at the Batalovs' for three days' and, when the two men visit the clinic, they ask if 'Semenova' is there. The device of leaving the characters 'nameless' suggests that they are prototypical, and was used later the same year by Lev Kuleshov in his triangle drama *Your Acquaintance* [Vasha znakomaia] also known as *The Journalist* [Zhurnalistka, 1927], in which the eponymous heroine, played by Alexandra Khokhlova, is called 'Khokhlova' and her modest admirer, played by Iu. Vasilchikov, is called 'Vasilchikov'. An attempt has been made to read the names in *Bed and Sofa* as a political allegory, with Nikolai doubling the last Tsar, Nicholas II, Vladimir doubling (Vladimir Ilich) Lenin, and the two of them battling over Liudmila ('*milaia liudiam*', dear to people) representing Russia, though this would seem to be a forced interpretation of a fortuitous combination of the actors' names.[41]

In *Bed and Sofa* the trio themselves address each other as 'Kolia', 'Liuda' and 'Volodia', the diminutives of their given names, Nikolai, Liudmila and Vladimir, and I shall use those names here.

The Film's Opening Sequence

Bed and Sofa opens with scenes of a railway track emerging from behind the speeding early morning train which is bearing Volodia to Moscow in search of work.[42] The mid-1920s was a time of large-

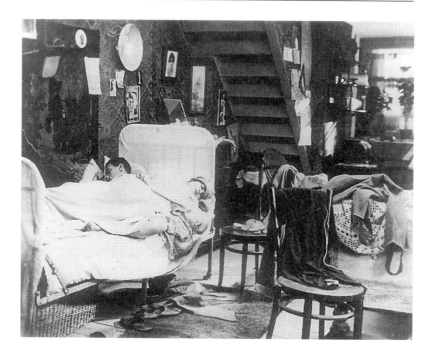

4. Kolia (Nikolai Batalov) and Liuda (Liudmila Semenova) lie in bed at the start of the film

scale migration to Moscow in search of a new life, and the motif is used to open other films of the period. In Barnet's *The Girl with the Hatbox* [Devushka s korobkoi, 1927], the young hero, Ilia Snegirev, takes the train from the provinces to Moscow to study at the Workers' Educational Faculty, while Parasha, the peasant heroine of his 1927 *The House on Trubnaia*, comes to find work as a domestic servant. The motif of the journey to Moscow would be canonised in the 1930s in the musicals of Grigori Alexandrov, where it would combine erotic fulfilment with ideological enlightenment in the political centre.

Shots of Volodia looking expectantly from the train window are intercut with the track and the couplings between carriages, and with plays of light and shadow. Volodia is immediately associated with light, speed and dynamism.[43] He is the first character seen in the film, and later his irruption into the flat, and the lives, of the other characters will be the catalyst for the film's plot.

The opening sequence develops into a montage of Volodia on the train, Moscow street life, and Kolia and Liuda in their semi-basement flat. The intertitle 'Moscow was still asleep' cues the first of several aerial views of the city, this one including the Kremlin and the Cathedral of Christ the Saviour, a building which at the period still dominated the Moscow skyline. It plays the same symbolic role in a scene in Boris Pasternak's *Doctor Zhivago*, in which Zhivago, returning to the city after the Revolution, catches sight of it from his train window, leading him to proclaim 'Moscow'.[44] It is succeeded by the titles 'Third Meshchanskaia is sleeping', and 'And its inhabitants', followed by Kolia and Liuda asleep in bed, facing in opposite directions, and a lamplighter putting out the lamp in the street outside. The next title, 'Moscow awoke', is followed by scenes of waking and washing, both in the city, where street sweepers are at work and a tram is being hosed down, and in the flat, where Liuda, Kolia and their cat perform their morning ablutions. All this intercutting suggests that the flat is a microcosm of the city, and this device too is used in a number of the films of the time. *The House on Trubnaia* starts with the intertitles 'The town is asleep', 'And the House on Trubnaia is asleep', and 'The town was waking up', and follows them with scenes of the town, and its inhabitants, waking and washing, sweeping and cleaning, scenes which are also present at the beginning of Vertov's *The Man with the Movie Camera* [Chelovek s kinoapparatom, 1928], a film which aims to provide a summation of life in the modern city.

The Flat: NEP and *Byt*

Most of *Bed and Sofa* takes place in the one-room flat on Third Meshchanskaia Street and the film's plot revolves around the changing functions of this domestic space. From the opening scenes it is apparent that the flat is cluttered: objects fill every available space and make it difficult for the characters to move around. As well as the bed and the sofa, the room will gradually be revealed to contain a rocking chair, a chest of drawers full of crockery, a mirror, a handsome wall clock, curtains cutting off the kitchen and the entrance hall, a dividing screen, a rug, a wicker case stowed under the bed, potted plants, a samovar, a teapot, a soup tureen, articles Kolia uses in his work and a number of little plaster ornaments. Clothes are strewn over the floor. A calendar and several pictures cover the walls, including a photograph of Liuda herself, portraits of Tolstoy, Stalin and Marshal Budenny, a picture of swans and a cover illustration from the film magazine *Sovetskii ekran* [Soviet Screen].[45]

In an early 1926 article 'My Cinema Convictions', Room had spoken of: 'That exceptional significance which must be given to the thing. In ordinary life things are *mute*, insignificant. They do not speak of anything and show no activity. In the cinema, on the screen, a thing grows to gigantic proportions and acts with the same force (if not a greater force) as man himself.'[46] This insight was developed in the interview he gave about *Bed and Sofa* (quoted above), in which he referred to the 'close captivity' in which things held the inhabitants of the flat. Shklovsky, too, considered the role of things in films to be paramount. In a piece published in *Kino* on 22 March 1927, exactly a week after the release of *Bed and Sofa*, he argued that the cinema was entering its 'second period', in which it would become 'a factory of the relationship with things', continuing: 'In the cinema in general you should not film things, what you have to do is to elucidate a relationship to them.' Taking Eisenstein's *The Old and the New* [Staroe i novoe, 1929, begun 1927] as a model of appropriate practice, he contended that, in it, 'Things are not simply filmed, they are not photographs and not symbols, they are signs, which evoke in the viewer their own semantic sequences.'[47]

The image of people in thrall to things goes back to, among others, Mayakovsky, who set his 1913 play *Vladimir Mayakovsky – A Tragedy* in a modern city in which 'soulless things have named themselves masters and are climbing up to erase us'.[48] In pre-Revolutionary cinema, an ostentatiously well-stocked interior was typical of the triumphant new business class, people like Khromova, the self-made millionairess factory owner in Evgeni Bauer's *A Life for a Life* [Zhizn' za zhizn', 1916].

After the Revolution, and especially with the introduction of NEP, a concern that conditions had not changed led to a battle to overcome the old *byt*. The word *byt*, which means 'way of life', had come, like *meshchanstvo*, to signify a philistine domination by possessions. The avant-garde were particularly vociferous in their attacks. In 1923 Sergei Tretiakov excoriated 'fat-bottomed bourgeois-*meshchanskii byt*' which affected 'the structure of feelings and actions' and which 'even the most powerful blows of the Revolution' had not been able to destroy, leaving man 'the slave of things'. In 1926 the critic Boris Arvatov opposed it to the life of the proletariat and linked it specifically to the 'art of the flat', singling out 'geraniums, canaries and curtains' as tell-tale signs of its presence, while Kazimir Malevich considered that the new proletarian art should avoid pictorial representations of 'everyday trash' altogether.[49]

Mayakovsky had concluded his poem 'About Rubbish' with the words:

> Philistine *byt* is more terrible than Wrangel.
> Quick
> Twist off the heads of the canaries –
> so that communism
> is not defeated by canaries.[50]

He continued the attack in his epic 1924 poem 'About That' [Pro eto], in which he unleashes a stream of rhetoric upon a smugly conformist NEP household, but his words bounce back against him, like peas off a wall.[51] That the cult of possessions can seduce even those who were previously in the political vanguard is apparent in Alexandra Kollontai's 1923 novel, *Vasilisa Malygina*. Vasilisa's husband, a former anarchist but now a 'Soviet director', has done well out of NEP and moved into an old mansion. When Vasilisa first sets foot in it, she is immediately discountenanced by the sofas and carpets, the mirror, the large clock and the still lifes in their gilded frames. Her unease turns to horror when he shows her the bedroom, with its 'genuine silk coverlet' on the bed, pink night lamp, full-length mirror for dressing and 'shelves for all your lingerie and hats and fripperies'. 'It was as if she had stepped into someone else's house; there were none of the things she actually needed, not even a table on which she could put her books and papers.'[52]

The Party, too, engaged in battles over the new Soviet interior. Above all it was to be light and airy, leaving no room for what Lenin called the 'dirt of the old world', and people were encouraged to whitewash walls and paint their furniture white.[53] The 1924 volume *Advice for the Proletarian Housewife* urged her: 'not to stuff the apartment with unnecessary extra furniture, not to hang useless rags for decoration. These things not only significantly reduce the amount of light, but also harbour dust containing all manner of parasites, and poison the home with throngs of tiny bacteria which are extremely harmful to one's health.'[54]

According to the painter El Lissitzky, the room of the future would be like 'the best kind of travelling suitcase', stripped of everything except a mattress, a folding chair, a table and a gramophone.[55] At the end of 1928 *Komsomol'skaia pravda* would launch a 'Down with domestic trash' campaign, challenging its readers to throw out their trinkets, take down their pictures and postcards, and report to the paper on their successes.[56]

Thus, the very darkness of the semi-basement flat on Third Mesh-chanskaia Street is an affront to the new order, and none of the objects with which it is cluttered is ideologically neutral. Worker viewers of the film would complain that the soup tureen and the metal glass holders [podstakanniki] were unproletarian, and the artist Vladimir Tatlin was about to declare war on the chest of drawers.[57] Rugs were considered unhygienic and took too much labour to keep clean.[58]

But the main ideological battle grounds were the bed and the sofa themselves. Rakhmetov, the ascetic hero of *What is to be Done?*, had slept on a strip of felt lined with nails. Eisenstein boasted of having slept on the mirrored door of a wardrobe after the Revolution,[59] and in the 'The Tsaritsa's bedroom' sequence at the end of his *October* [Oktiabr', 1927], the ripping of the royal mattress by a sailor from the Amur Fleet is shown as a synecdoche of the revolutionary explosion as a whole. The new 'revolutionary' bed was to be multi-functional, easily folded away and invisible.[60] The *gorka*, the pile of well-stuffed pillows that before the Revolution had signified prosperity, was speci-fically rejected.[61] These pillows had played a memorable role in Nikolai Larin's 1913 film melodrama *Merchant Bashkirov's Daughter* [Doch' kuptsa Bashkirova], where they suffocated the 'unsuitable' suitor, but Liuda in *Bed and Sofa* ritually plumps them up each morning.

The sofa, too, is usually represented as an article of luxury. The protagonists of *What is to be Done?* only occasionally allow themselves to relax on one. Walter Benjamin describes a well-cushioned sofa as an essential feature of the *petit-bourgeois* NEP interior, and Svetlana Boym stresses that in post-Revolutionary households they were both rare and ideologically suspect.[62] Thus the very presence of the sofa in Room's film is yet another indicator of the slide back into *byt*, though it has to be said that the sofa here is not only the sleeping place of the sexual loser, but also both small and uncomfortable, only marginally more acceptable than the office desk.

Kolia

Kolia awakes with a broad smile and removes and reads the page from a tear-off calendar which announces that it is the third of the month. His instructions to his wife will establish that it is a Saturday and later intertitles that the month is July. The 3rd of July was indeed a Saturday in 1926,[63] so the film opens with a precise temporal orientation, and the several later intertitle references to time make it possible to date the events in the film precisely and to see that they almost exactly mirror the period in which the film was shot. Time, for Kolia, is a reliable, regular process.

Next, he washes and exercises. His ablutions, under a shower improvised from the samovar and standing in a bowl, are ostentatiously contrasted with Liuda's snatched face-wash at the kitchen tap. As the camera lingers on his naked torso, Kolia's narcissism becomes apparent. This early morning ritual of washing and exercises with weights immediately suggests that Kolia is a former military man, something that is confirmed by a quick intercut shot of the picture of Marshal Budenny, the Commander of the First Red Cavalry Army, pinned on the wall.[64] It will later be referred to explicitly.

The association of the 'new man' with physical exercise went back a long way. Rakhmetov, in Chernyshevsky's *What is to be Done?*, combines voracious reading to educate his mind with a programme of gymnastics and a diet of raw beef steak to build up his body.[65] The artists of Russian Modernism were also preoccupied with the design of a perfect body, and combined a cult of bodily exposure and display with a desire for the transformation of mankind.[66] Physical 'drill' exercises had been introduced in Russian schools from the 1870s to prepare boys for military service, but it was the Red Army that developed programmes of physical training on a grand scale. After the passing of a resolution 'On the Compulsory Teaching of the Military Arts' on 22 April 1918, the Central Board of Universal

Military Training (Vseobshchee voennoe obuchenie, Vsevobuch) was set up on 7 May 1918 to train conscripts through a programme of gymnastic exercises, barbells and hoops. The new regime increasingly associated physical fitness, health and good hygiene with political awareness and cultural enlightenment. Civil War slogans included 'Help the Country by Washing in Cold Water', 'Help the Country with a Toothbrush', and 'Physical Culture 24 Hours a Day!' The Komsomol concerned itself directly with the physical training of young people and organised local sporting circles. In the summer of 1925, the Party issued a decree 'On the Tasks of the Party in the Area of Physical Culture'.[67] Physical exercise was also propagandised in Mikhail Doronin's agit-film of 1926 *People Who were Once Somebody* [Byvshie liudi], in which a factory that uses its break time for physical exercises has a far higher production output than another that does not; but the cult of the body was parodied in the revolting morning gymnastics of the gross Soviet functionary and sausage-maker Andrei Babichev at the opening of Iuri Olesha's 1927 novel *Envy* [Zavist'].

Physical exercise was overwhelmingly associated with men. In 1921, only 4 per cent of Vsevobuch members were women,[68] and the healthy, exercising figures in the posters that supported the physical fitness campaign were almost invariably male,[69] though women exercise and participate in sport on a par with men in Vertov's *The Man with the Movie Camera*.

Kolia's Soviet credentials are further confirmed by his reading the *Rabochaia gazeta* [Workers' Paper] as he eats his breakfast and has his first morning cigarette. After this, instructing Liuda to pass him the sheaf of working drawings he has forgotten and reminding her that 'Today is Saturday – don't forget to wash the floors', he departs for work.

It is at this point that we learn that 'He was working as a foreman [desiatnik] on the Bolshoi Theatre', which is under reconstruction. Just as he presides and gives orders at home, so he presides at work. The rhetoric of construction was widespread in the 1920s and, after the Fourteenth Party Congress in December 1925 had set the course for 'socialist industrialisation', a number of grandiose projects were undertaken in Moscow. Mayakovsky, in 'Two Moscows' [Dve Moskvy], a poem published in *Izvestiia TsIK* on 12 September 1926, while the film was being shot, contrasts 'snoring old Moscow' with the scaffolding on the towering new buildings of the Central Tele-graph Office and the Lenin Institute.[70] Both of these construction sites are shown in the exterior sequences of *Bed and Sofa*, yet Room chooses to have Kolia work on the Bolshoi, a building symbolic of the cultural past. Lenin had referred to it as 'a little piece of land-owner culture',[71] while Vertov, in *The Man with the Movie Camera*, would use a split screen to blow the building apart.[72] Kolia is supervising its reconstruction. The classical sculpture on the top of the pediment of the building depicts Apollo and a team of four horses. After setting his men to work, Kolia eats his lunch on the back of one of the horses. Then he reclines against the genitals of the naked Apollo, has another cigarette and stretches contentedly.[73] This connection with the Greek god who in art represents the ideal of youthful manly beauty is further evidence of Kolia's masculine self-satisfaction.[74]

When Kolia rushes to leave at the end of his shift, a colleague asks him, 'Where are you going? There's a meeting now', to which Kolia replies, 'Oh, why? ... I'd rather go home.' Meetings were, indeed, the bane of contemporary life. Walter Benjamin, in the city at the time, noted that:

> For each citizen of Moscow the days are full to the brim. Meetings, committees are fixed at all hours in offices, clubs, factories, and often have no site of their own, being held in corners of noisy editorial rooms, at the cleared table of a canteen. There is a kind of natural selection and a struggle for existence between these meetings.[75]

The solution suggested by Mayakovsky was that citizens should cut themselves in half and attend twice as many meetings in the same time.[76] Nevertheless, attendance at such meetings was considered a potent ideological and social glue, integrating the citizen into the work of the collective. Addressing the Sixth Congress of the Komsomol in 1924, Nadezhda Krupskaia, Lenin's widow, insisted: 'We understand perfectly well that personal life cannot be separated from social concerns. Perhaps earlier it was not clear that a division between private life and public life sooner or later leads to the betrayal of communism. We must strive to bind our private life to the struggle for and the construction of communism.'[77]

A year later, Liadov, the Rector of the Sverdlov Communist

University, asserted in his book *Questions of Daily Life* [Voprosy byta], 'We imagine the society of the future as one in which everyone will feel that his interests conform with the interests of the entire collective',[78] while the Commissar for Health, Nikolai Semashko, stressed that: 'The petit bourgeois turns his back on all manner of social life (what use is it to him?); he lives only for the interest of his own comfort [uiut], his clothing; the miserable happiness of his family is the goal of his life.'[79]

Thus, though Kolia is outwardly a representative of the new order, both through his status as a builder and through his military past, his attitudes and behaviour show that he is also still prey to the etiolating pull of the past.

Liuda

The Revolution heralded sweeping changes in the formal status of women.[80] An All-Russian Congress of Women, held in 1918, led to the establishment, in December of that year, of commissions for propaganda and agitation among women workers, with a central commission headed by Inessa Armand. In September 1919 the commission was upgraded into the Zhenotdel [Zhenotdel TsK RKP(b), the Women's Department of the Central Committee of the Russian Communist Party (Bolshevik)], again initially headed by Armand, and then, from 1920 to 1922, by Kollontai. The tasks of the Zhenotdel were set out in a number of Central Committee resolutions, and stressed in particular the political education of women workers and peasants and drawing them into Party, professional and co-operative institutions.[81] They were also articulated in the forthright statements of the women who ran the organisation. In a lecture given at the Sverdlov University in 1921, Kollontai spoke in favour of the establishment of state-run dining rooms, of house communes, and of the state upbringing of children, thus releasing more women into the workforce, since Soviet power needed women's work to be of use to the whole state, and not just to their home and family. The liberation of women would be accomplished as part of the radical reformation of life as a whole.[82] In the words of Barbara Evans Clements, the leaders of Zhenotdel were driven by a utopian vision, the key feature of which was:

the creation of a 'new woman' whose defining characteristics were independence and activism. Zhenotdel writers portrayed her as a true believer and a revolutionary fighter who was, as one propagandist stated, 'a human being, the builder of a new life' [...] 'A strong, free citizen, not inferior to man in anything', she was politically and legally equal to any man. She was as fully involved as any man in the productive work of the world beyond the family [...] Putilovskaia, a Zhenotdel worker, happily summed up the credo in 1920: 'Communism emancipates women [...] transforms woman from the "wife of a person" into a person.'[83]

So the new Soviet woman would be active, both in work, politics and study, and in the organisation of her own life. In the words of a woman worker, '*Men cannot defend our interests*; they don't understand us.'[84] In the art of the period, too, predominance was given to the active woman, directly participating in the life and fate of the country. The taxonomy of the peasant, proletarian and fighter heroines of the Soviet fiction of the period provided by Xenia Gasiorowska confirms this reading,[85] while among the most memorable heroines of the first decade of Soviet cinema are Pelageia Vlasova, the heroine of Pudovkin's version of Gorky's novel *The Mother* [Mat′, 1926], moved to political activism by the fate of her son, and Mariutka, the heroine of Iakov Protazanov's 1926 version of Boris Lavrenev's story *The Forty-First* [Sorok pervyi], who sacrifices the personal to the cause and shoots the White officer with whom she has fallen in love.[86]

Yet under NEP the opportunities women had for active participation in social life were severely curtailed and 'the sense of limitless possibilities [...] began to ebb'.[87] For one thing, there was a huge increase in female unemployment as millions of men, who had greater work experience and a wider range of skills, flocked to the cities after demobilisation at the end of the Civil War. The 1926 census showed that over half the adult women in Moscow were economically dependent, despite the fact that Moscow was a centre for the textile industry and was now the seat of government. The census also revealed that 72 per cent of Moscow households had only one member who was working or seeking work and that 80 per cent of households were headed by a male.[88] The Party was predominantly interested in women as a productive part of the workforce, less in the reconstruction of their personal and family lives. At the same time, women's experience of official organisations such as the Komsomol was that they frequently failed to understand the women's perspective.[89]

Describing the plots of 1920s fiction about proletarian life, Gasiorowska stresses that the male protagonist is shown mainly at his workplace, whereas, 'His wife, if she stayed at home, was as impersonal as she had been in prerevolutionary fiction, and her role just as insignificant, because she was outside the mainstream of the plot'.[90] This is consistent with our first impressions of Liuda in *Bed and Sofa*. In the film's opening montage sequences she is almost invisible. As the camera concentrates on the peregrinations of Kolia and Volodia about the city, she is confined to the inner space. It is also particularly striking, and surely polemically intended by Shklovsky and Room, that in a period when so much attention was being directed to drawing women into collective life she is completely isolated. She has no friend or neighbour, no job, no link to any Party organisations and structures, and seemingly no consciousness of them. Thus she is outside all official Soviet systems, neither a negative nor a positive character, merely passive.

Even within the space of the flat she is marginalised, continually retreating to the kitchen. One of the film's posters, designed by Vladimir and Georgi Stenberg, shows her looking out from behind its lace curtain, and she is repeatedly associated with images of enclosure and framing. The fundamental importance of the lack of their own individual space to the continuing subjugation of women was recognised by Chernyshevsky. In *What is to be Done?* Lopukhov and Vera Pavlovna have separate rooms to ensure both their privacy and their sexual equality.[91] Kollontai's Vasilisa Malygina would have left her feckless husband far earlier if only she had been able to find a room of her own.[92] And at the other end of Europe, in two papers delivered in Cambridge the year after *Bed and Sofa* was made, Virginia Woolf, concerned with the question of why historically so few women had become writers, stressed the crucial need to assure women's autonomy by spatial and financial independence: 'give her a room of her own and five hundred a year'.[93]

The sense that Liuda is imprisoned in this space is underlined by the frequency with which she is shown standing or sitting at the window. This is the traditional pose of the aspirant Romantic heroine,

5. Poster for the film designed by Vladimir and Georgi Stenberg, 1927

and is the place where Pushkin's Tatiana spends entire days in *Eugene Onegin*, but Liuda has no view of sylvan landscapes.[94] Rather, in a stark case of what Darrell William Davis has called the 'perceptual reorganisation engendered by city life', her vista, impeded by curtain and by semi-basement, is restricted to the feet of passers-by and the wheels of cars.[95]

Confined in her basement, Liuda occupies herself with housework, a task in which she is completely unaided. The subjugation of women to domestic chores preoccupied Party thinkers. In a famous and widely anthologised conversation of 1920 with the German communist head of the women's secretariat of the Comintern, Klara Zetkin, Lenin said:

> Very few husbands, not even among the proletarians, think of how much they could lighten the burdens and worries of their wives or even remove them entirely, if they would only lend a hand in 'woman's work'. But no, after all this is repellent to 'the right and honour of the husband'. He demands that he should have rest and comfort. The domestic life of the woman is a daily self-sacrifice through thousands of insignificant trifles. The old right of dominion of the husband continues to live in a hidden way. His slave objectively avenges herself for this – also in a hidden way: the backwardness of the woman, her lack of understanding of the revolutionary ideals of her husband, weakens his spirits and decisiveness in the struggle [...] Our communist work among the female masses, our political work, includes within it a significant amount of educational work among men. We must stamp out the old slave-owning point of view to its last and tiniest roots. Both in the party and in the masses.[96]

Trotsky, too, in his article 'From the Old Family to the New', published in *Pravda* on 13 July 1923, had insisted that 'As long as woman is chained to her housework, the care of the family, the cooking and sewing, all her chances of participation in social and political life are cut down in the extreme', while admitting that the reform of the family was more arduous than the achievement of either political or industrial equality and that the state could not yet afford the socialisation of family housekeeping.[97] Kollontai, in a speech given at the All-Russian Congress of Women in 1918, had gone so far as to subdivide women's domestic labour into four component parts – cleaning, cooking, washing and mending – before suggesting that all of this could be taken over by social management, leading to the 'death' of housework.[98] Alas, almost a decade later Liuda is seen engaged in all four of these activities.

There are already some signs of Liuda's dissatisfaction with her lot, expressed by her imprecation 'Husband!' [Muzh!] as she stubs out Kolia's cigarette after he has left for work, but at this stage she seems resigned, complicit in her own subjection.[99] In a brief return to her at the end of the opening sequence we see that she has dutifully prepared dinner (her cookbook is still in evidence). Arranging it attractively on the table, she combs her hair and prepares to change into a pretty dress for her husband's return. In the words of Liudmila Semenova, Liuda at this stage 'accepted everything that was happening as inevitable, seeing no way out and resigning herself to her fate'. Semenova saw Liuda as a typical woman of the period, and, without either 'correcting' or 'idealising' her, intended to play the role in such a way as to 'arouse in many women a sense of protest against their subjection within the family', insisting that the 'restraint and sparse actorly means' she had learnt from Kozintsev and Trauberg were very useful to this end.[100]

Kolia and Liuda

The model NEP couple is represented by Gusev, another former Red Army man and member of Budenny's army (also played by Nikolai Batalov), and his wife Masha, a nurse, in Iakov Protazanov's 1924 film *Aelita*. Though they go through struggles, and Gusev initially fails to adapt to the new order, they overcome them, and both husband and wife are seen to have their role to play. After Gusev saves the country in war, Masha nurses it, and him, back to health. Alas, relations between Kolia and Liuda fall far short of this ideal. For one thing, Kolia seems driven to treat his wife with a petty childish sadism. While she is still asleep he throws the cat on her face.[101] After he reads the page of the calendar he screws it up and flicks it at her. When she serves him hot milk he first complains that there is no holder for the glass and then scrapes off the skin at the top of the milk and sticks it under her nose. Later he will repeatedly subject her to humiliating practical jokes.

Kolia gives orders and Liuda carries them out. While he does his exercises she carries the samovar off to fill it with water for his shower. While she cooks, he eats. When he leaves, he gives instructions for the day. As Lenin had told Zetkin:

> Unfortunately, one might still say of several of our comrades: 'Scratch a communist and you will find a philistine.' Of course you should scratch a sensitive spot – his psyche with regard to women. Is there any more graphic proof of this than the fact that men look calmly on while women wear themselves out in petty, monotonous and exhausting housework, which devours their time and strength [...]?[102]

These family relations are also expressed spatially. Within the flat, Kolia sits contentedly at the table while Liuda skulks in the kitchen. Later, he goes out and she stays in. He looks down, the master of all he surveys, she looks up, mistress of nothing. In the words of Virginia Woolf, 'women have sat indoors all these millions of years'.[103] It is remarkable that the internal and external spatial relations of *Bed and Sofa* also replicate exactly the mores of a pre-revolutionary provincial merchant household in Nikolai Larin's *Merchant Bashkirov's Daughter*. There, too, the husband presides at the table, where he is later joined by his friend and double, while his wife and daughter serve the food and then hover in the margins of the room and the film frame. There, too, the man goes brightly out to work, and the women are confined to the house. But whereas in *Merchant Bashkirov's Daughter* the emergence of the heroine into the world presages disaster, the plot of *Bed and Sofa*, and the liberation of its heroine, are expressed through her ever more confident and determined move into outside space.

Volodia

Arriving at the Briansk station,[104] Volodia walks around the city in search of work. He consults a map and passes several Moscow landmarks. His actions continue to be edited into the scenes inside the flat, and directly after Liuda complains, 'Husband!', Volodia kicks a stone into water and makes ripples, presaging the effect of his entrance into the couple's lives. He signs up for work at the printers of the *Rabochaia gazeta*, the paper Kolia is reading at breakfast, but is told that he must arrange somewhere to live for himself. As he walks around, we note that physically he is the antithesis of Kolia, thin and wiry, forever in motion, unlike his more solidly built friend. He passes near the Kremlin and by the Bolshoi where Kolia is working. He sits on a bench in a little square opposite the Moscow City Soviet building near the Freedom Obelisk. This is the fullest picture of Moscow topography the film will provide. Thus, though Volodia is an outsider, he is immediately shown to be at ease in Moscow, and all the movings about the city are associated predominantly with him.[105]

And then, unexpectedly, he bursts in on Liuda.

Kolia, Liuda and Volodia

As Liuda insists 'You can't come in here. This is a private flat', the cane chair behind which she is skulking makes a pattern of light and shade on her face.[106] But this is not some marauder, merely one of the little tricks with which Kolia likes to surprise his wife. With the words, 'Don't be shy, Volodia', Kolia introduces him, explaining, 'It's Fogel, an old friend. We sheltered under a single greatcoat in the war … we fought in the Red Army together … I ran into him in the square', and kisses him in greeting. There is another flash of the picture of Budenny on the wall. Red Army service during the Civil War was accepted as a 'formative proletarian experience',[107] and the tendency to idealise the male exploits and male comradeship of the war years increased in the less stirring times of NEP.[108] Women, in consequence, were substantially erased from the iconography of the Civil War period.[109]

Kolia sets Volodia and his portmanteau down on the sofa with the words, 'Well, friend, don't stand on ceremony … the sofa is your kingdom.' He has not consulted Liuda, since he is 'master' of this space, and he makes the decisions. He finds a screen in the entrance hall which will further break up the living area and push her further to the margins.

The next scene shows Volodia at work at the printers of *Rabochaia gazeta*. A montage of the process of printing again associates Volodia with energy, dynamism and speed – his hair stands on end from the static electricity – and he is shown to be, like Kolia, a skilled and responsible worker.[110]

6. The yardman (Leonid Iurenev)

Three days later, the cat lies on the sofa, while Liuda, in a head-scarf, is busy doing the washing. She has a visit from the bearded old yardman, played by Leonid Iurenev, his cap badge, with its number, 768, indicating his official duties. He hands her Volodia's passport and casts a quizzical eye upon the sofa. He tells Liuda that he has registered Volodia in the flat, 'but without the right to living space'. To his further question, 'Where does he work?', Liuda, who still seems quite indifferent to Volodia's presence, replies, 'He lives on our sofa, and he works as a printer'.

The question of the 'living space' to which each Soviet employee was entitled had been referred to by Room in the statement he made before the film. Two weeks after the Revolution, Lenin had sketched out a project for the 'requisition of the flats of the rich to relieve the need of the poor', and a rich flat was considered any one in which 'the number of rooms is equal to or greater than the number of permanent inhabitants of the flat'.[111] New inhabitants were also settled into flats that were considered under-occupied, a process whose name provides the title of one of the first Soviet films, Aleksandr Panteleev's *Consolidation of Living Space* [Uplotnenie], released for the first anniversary of the Revolution on 7 November 1918. Panteleev offers an idyllic reading of the enforced resettlement. A worker and his daughter are transferred from a damp basement into a room in the flat of a professor of chemistry at Petrograd University. For a while the professor's wife and son are uneasy but within a short time the professor begins to give lectures in the Workers' Club and the daughter of the workman and the son of the professor fall in love. The reaction of Professor Preobrazhensky, in Mikhail Bulgakov's 1925 novella *The Heart of a Dog* [Sobach'e serdtse], is altogether more jaundiced. When the house committee insists that he must have someone settled into his flat, he retorts that his existing seven rooms are not enough and that he needs a library. When they ask him to give up his dining room, stressing that no one in Moscow now has one, 'not even Isadora Duncan', he is driven to fury:

> To take my food in the bedroom – he began in a rather strangled voice – to read in the consulting room, to dress in the drawing room, to operate in the maid's room and to examine people in the dining room?! It is very possible that this is what Isadora Duncan does. Maybe she dines in her study and cuts up rabbits in her bathroom. Maybe. But I am not Isadora Duncan!![112]

The destruction of the war years, the lack of funds and the huge wave of urban immigration had put enormous pressure on the housing stock. Officially each citizen was allowed a 'living sanitary norm' of 8.25 sq. m, but the 1926 census showed that the average in practice was only 5.9 sq. m and among workers only 4.99.[113] Though some attempts were made to address the situation by co-operative building, P. Kozhany, a leading writer on the subject, described the living conditions of workers in 1925 as 'thoroughly dreadful'.[114]

NEP survivors used every means possible to hold on to their extra space. Madame Irene, the shop-owning employer of Natasha, the heroine of *The Girl with the Hatbox*, does so by falsely registering Natasha in a room in her flat. Meanwhile, Natasha's poor student admirer is reduced to sleeping in a station waiting room, but eventually the young couple marry and assert their right to the space. The hunt for living space became a fixation. As Woland says of Muscovites in Bulgakov's *The Master and Margarita*: 'they're people like any others [...] ordinary people ... In general they're like people used to be ... it's just that the question of flats has ruined them.'[115] Walter Benjamin, referring to the creation of communal apartments, considered that 'Bolshevism has abolished private life', and noted that the scarcity of living quarters meant that in the evenings almost every window, large or small, had a light in it.[116] In this context, Liuda's horrified imprecation, 'You can't come in here. This is a private flat', is understandable, as is the fact that Volodia cannot be allotted any 'living space'.

The next intertitle announces that it is the morning of the 9th of July, six days after Volodia's arrival. Liuda is at work as usual, folding away the screen and preparing to make the bed, when Volodia arrives from the night shift with a parcel of gifts, the first of them a radio, the second a copy of the magazine *Novyi mir*. In *What is to be Done?* Lopukhov brings Vera Pavlovna two books, Considérant's *Destinée sociale* and Feuerbach's *Lectures on the Essence of Religion*, the 'enlightening' effect of which is both intended and immediate.[117] Volodia's gifts are also ideologically significant, both of them tools by which the new regime can disseminate information and propaganda, a process in which Volodia is directly involved through his job at the printers. Both Lenin and Stalin had used radio during the days of Revolution, and in 1920 Lenin called it, 'a newspaper without paper and without distance' and 'a great enterprise'. Experimental radio broadcasts began in September 1922, regular ones from 1924.[118] When at the end of Lev Kuleshov's *The Extraordinary Adventures of Mr West in the Land of the Bolsheviks* the hero sends a radio message to inform his wife of his ideological maturation, we see it transmitted by the enormous Shukhov Radio Tower, which had been constructed in 1919–22 and which would later so impress Walter Benjamin.[119] The Society of Friends of Soviet Cinema had a slogan, 'The cinema and the radio into the village and the workers' quarters',[120] and Dziga Vertov referred to its propaganda power in a number of articles and included radio broadcasts in a number of his films.[121] Sergei Iutkevich and S. Griunberg co-directed an agit-film called *You Give us Radio!* [Daesh´ radio!] in 1925, while in the same year, in Semen Timoshenko's *Radio Detective* [Radiodetektiv], radio is used to catch a NEPman who has refused to pay his taxes.

Liuda shows a polite interest in the radio and turns to get on with her chores, but it is the second gift which particularly interests her. She stops making the bed and cuts the pages – which Volodia has significantly left uncut – with a penknife she conveniently has in her pocket. The monthly journal *Novyi mir*, which combined literary with socio-political material, had been published in Moscow from 1925, and at regular intervals throughout Soviet history would be connected with liberal tendencies, but it is not, of course, this which interests Liuda. What excites her is the title on the cover, *New World*, a point underlined by the appearance of the words as an intertitle. Volodia watches her reaction attentively, and then, to her amazed pleasure, clears the table and folds away the tablecloth. She leans against the pillows reading while Volodia busies himself around the flat, directly reversing the breakfast scene of the start of the film. Is this unprecedented male helpfulness or the tactics of seduction? – neither Liuda nor the viewer is yet sure.

Volodia and Liuda

The film cuts to a scene of Kolia at work. He receives a telegram, telling him he must catch a train in twenty minutes. Back at the flat he sees Volodia lying on the sofa, and Liuda lying on the bed, reading *Novyi mir*, but he is too taken up with his own affairs to take in the extraordinariness of the scene. Volodia overhears Kolia tell Liuda, 'Quick, I'm going on a business trip' – Kolia is going out into communist construction, just as the engineer Los does in *Aelita* – and

7. Volodia (Vladimir Fogel) and Kolia, before Kolia's departure on business

calls him over. Uncertain how to tie his case, Kolia leaves the packing to Liuda and goes to sit on the sofa with Volodia. Volodia insists that he will move out, that it would not be appropriate for him to stay in Kolia's absence, that tongues would wag. Kolia finds such a suggestion hilarious, and after an intercut shot of Liuda folding and packing his clothes he says: 'You're joking, brother. No one will take her from me.' He feels Volodia's biceps, flexes his own, which are considerably more developed, and adds, cryptically, 'I'm not ticklish'. Once again a decision affecting Liuda's future is being made without her involvement, once again she is an eavesdropper on her own life; and catching sight of Kolia's antics, she diverts her fury into frenzied packing. Kolia and Volodia shake hands, and Liuda sits pensively leaning on the case, her hands to her mouth. Kolia leaves, kissing and admonishing her on his way. Volodia turns his face to the wall and goes back to sleep. Liuda sits over *Novyi mir*, but she can no longer concentrate.

8. Liuda packs for Kolia

An intertitle takes us to 'The 14th of July. Aviakhim day'. Aviakhim, the Society of the Friends of Aviation and Chemical Construction, had been formed in May 1925, with the amalgamation of the Society of the Friends of the Air Fleet [Obshchestvo druzei vozdushnogo flota], founded in March 1923, and the Society of the Friends of Chemistry [Dobrokhim], set up a year later. Formally 'volunteer' organisations, they were in fact officially run and had the aim of providing elementary programmes of military training and chemical and aviation technology for the masses. Closely linked to the Soviet armed forces, they had a predominantly male membership. In January 1927 they would be combined with the Military Scientific

Society [Voenno-nauchnoe obshchestvo] to form the Society of Friends of Defence, Aviation and Chemical Construction [Osoviakhim].[122]

We see rows of planes, men marching, an aerial display, and then men in gas-masks emerging from clouds of smoke.[123] Volodia has brought Liuda to the celebrations, and takes her for a ride in a plane, on the side of which are the words 'Agit-Plane of the Society of the Friends of Aviation and Chemical Construction of the Russian Soviet Federative Socialist Republic'. This is the first time Liuda has been in a plane and her excitement is palpable. Initially chaperoned by Volodia, she makes him swap places and let her sit at the window. Later, after a snatched tram-ride through Moscow (in which Volodia and Liuda are not seen – Liuda is not seen in the open spaces of the city at any point in the film) they go to the cinema, another treat for Liuda, who cannot remember when she was last there.

So Volodia has taken her out into the world, 'broadened her horizons'. The views they have from the plane are far higher than those of Kolia at the top of the Bolshoi. Yet this whole sequence is organised by Volodia, and in it Liuda remains an outsider, a spectator. The window of the flat is replaced by the window of the plane. Instead of looking up at people's feet, she looks down, and from such a distance that people are not visible at all.[124] She preserves her observer status in the darkened cinema, and this scene is so brief that we do not even catch sight of the film that they watch.

Back in the flat, Volodia helps her off with her jacket and, while she is combing her hair, their eyes meet in the mirror, which frames her as the object of his gaze. We can see her photograph on the wall along with the illustration of the cover star of *Sovetskii ekran*. Liuda is wearing a pretty white blouse. He smoothes her hair, cut fashionably short, and tells her something the viewer has long since noticed, 'You know ... you're pretty' [vy khoroshen'kaia], but at this point she rebuffs his advances. He moves to the sofa, the wall above it now decorated with his pictures – is this acceptance of defeat or tactics? The cat is lying on the sofa and Volodia, watching Liuda closely, sees that she has taken up a pack of cards. Though there is no clear indication that she is doing so – she may be about to lay out a game of patience – he asks her: 'Are you telling your fortune? ... would you like me to tell it for you?'

In Russian culture, telling your fortune at cards was a female

9. Liuda reassembles the cards

10. Poster for the film designed by Iakov Ruklevsky, 1927

pastime. There are several examples of it in nineteenth-century literature. In Pushkin's 1829 poem 'It's Winter. What can we do in the
country?' [Zima. Chto delat' nam v derevne?], while men talk of the
forthcoming election and the local sugar mill, the bored hostess either
knits or 'tells fortunes from the King of Hearts'. Pushkin's Tatiana
and Goncharov's Olga in *Oblomov* tell their fortune from cards, and
the heroine of Gogol's play *Marriage* [Zhenit'ba] uses them to decide
on her marriage prospects.[125]

Liuda's turn to the cards *may* imply a new uncertainty about her
future, but Volodia does not intend to leave things to chance. First he
selects for Liuda the Queen of Hearts.[126] Then he says, 'Now let's see
what's in [literally 'on'] your heart'. By a sleight of hand he finds the
Jack of Diamonds and signals his intentions by covering the Queen
with the Jack. Volodia's choice for himself of the Jack of Diamonds
shows that he is fully aware of the implications of his actions. In
France from the seventeenth century the Jack of Diamonds [le valet
de carreau] had come to signify a scoundrel, and the usage spread
from there to Russia. Its errant implications were embraced by the
painters Mikhail Larionov and Aristarkh Lentulov for the name of
the group of avant-garde painters they founded in 1910 after they

had been expelled from the Moscow Institute of Painting, Architecture and Sculpture for rebelliousness and leftism. In Dostoevsky's novel *The Idiot*, Gania Ivolgin tells Prince Myshkin that Nastasia Filippovna 'is going to consider me a Jack of Diamonds [za valeta bubnovogo] all her life', adding, 'Why does everyone copy her and call me a scoundrel?'[127] Scoundrel [podlets] is precisely the word that Volodia will use to Kolia at the end of the film to characterise their behaviour.

The next scene shows them both on the bed. Volodia is asleep, his face buried in the pillows. Liuda is sitting wide awake, her head against the iron head rail. A wind rustles the curtain at the open window, and blows the Jack off the Queen. A momentary blurring of the image suggests Liuda's confusion. She turns to see that Volodia is still wearing his shoes, and gives a sardonic shrug. She sits deep in thought, even biting the iron bedrail. She gets up, goes back to the table, searches through the cards and places the King of Hearts next to the Queen, then shifts the Queen of Hearts so that it is midway between the King of Hearts and the Jack of Diamonds. And so they lie: King, Queen, Knave.[128] The importance of this sequence is indicated by the fact that one of the film's contemporary posters, designed by Iakov Ruklevsky, shows the Jack, Queen and King stylised with the actors' heads.[129]

Volodia shifts in his sleep and Liuda moves the pillow to make him more comfortable. He awakes, yawns and takes her hand, asking, 'What about Kolia?' Emboldened by her silence, he adds, 'Does that mean ... ?' He moves his pillows from the sofa to the bed. They shake hands and an intertitle announces, 'Welcome to your new home!' [S novosel'em!] This move to the marital bed and the handshake suggest that Liuda and Kolia consider themselves to have embarked upon what was known at the time as a 'de facto' (unregistered) marriage [fakticheskii brak].

There had been several changes to the legal status of marriage since the Revolution. Decrees on civil marriage and on divorce, passed in December 1917, meant that henceforth only civil marriages, registered in state registry offices [ZAGS] would be recognised, and established that either husband or wife could ask for a divorce. They were developed into the First Code of Laws on Marriage, the Family and Guardianship, in October 1918.[130] Discussion of the marriage code

11. Volodia and Liuda embark upon their relationship

then continued throughout the early 1920s. Various drafts were drawn up, leading to a final draft in October 1925 which, after a year of very wide public discussion and further amendment, was ratified by the Central Executive Committee as the Code of Laws on Marriage, the Family and the Right of Guardianship in November 1926 and passed into law in January 1927. Among its crucial provisions were those concerning the recognition of de facto marriages, joint rights to property acquired during the marriage, the simplification of divorce procedures, the duties of fathers, the determination of disputed paternity and the provision of alimony.[131] The extension of rights to those in de facto marriages, a widespread consequence of NEP, was warmly supported by urban women.

An intertitle reports that a few more days have passed, though the calendar remains on the 9th.[132] Liuda sits in the rocking chair and sews a button on Volodia's shirt collar. This action, too, has ideological significance. Lenin's wife Krupskaia recalls attending a young people's debate about sexual equality during the revolutionary period.

Attention had focused on whether men should learn to sew. When one young man argued that there was no need for this, since girls could already do so, there was a storm of protest. Reminded that, 'A wife is a comrade to her husband, and not a servant!', he was forced to give way.[133]

Liuda's actions are intercut with scenes of Volodia at work, but he is staring pensively into space. The patterning of light and shade cast on his face by the printing machine directly echoes that which the cane rocking chair had cast on Liuda's face when Volodia first came to the flat, thus further stressing the link between them.[134] Each is thinking of the other, but the sexual division of labour – male paid work outside the flat, traditional female 'housework' within it – has not been disturbed.

Kolia's Return

Suddenly, as Liuda sits rocking in the chair, the flat door opens. 'Stop, don't move!' shouts Kolia, his arm outstretched. Both Liuda and the viewer of course think that Kolia 'knows'. In fact, however, this is just another of his little 'tricks'. He turns away and returns with a large pannier of berries: 'See what a husband you have. You can make us some jam.' For the second time in the film, the word 'husband' is associated with an order to perform a household chore, this time by Kolia himself. Liuda trembles in a mixture of relief and irritation.

Scenes of Volodia finishing work are intercut with Kolia replacing his work instruments on the wall of the flat. Noticing that the calendar still says the 9th, he tears off a further nine days, up to the 18th, and says, 'What, did time stand still without me?', utterly innocent of the import of his remark. Liuda makes the jam and Kolia supervises. Hearing Volodia's return he cannot resist another tease. As Volodia puts some shopping on the table, Kolia places his hands over his eyes. Volodia smiles, strokes a hand and turns to kiss the proffered lips. Liuda watches from behind the curtain. Kolia bursts into raucous laughter. Volodia is amazed, but Liuda, too, grins from behind the curtain. Kolia offers Volodia a manly handshake and asks, 'How do you like our sofa?'

Liuda emerges with a large soup tureen and calls them to dinner. Kolia eats in high spirits, while Volodia looks sheepishly at the paper and Liuda becomes increasingly uneasy. Suddenly Kolia tells Liuda, 'I've only just noticed how pretty you are' [kakaia ty u menia khoroshen'kaia]. The use of the possessive [u menia] and of the very word, 'pretty', [khoroshen'kaia], that Volodia had used in his seduction discountenances Liuda, and she leaves the table. Kolia turns to Volodia: 'It's true, isn't it, Liuda is pretty?'

As Liuda listens from behind the gauze curtain, Volodia is embarrassed into a confession: 'Kolia ... I have to tell you ... that your wife and I ... ' This is a profound shock to Kolia. He twists and stabs his fork, he stands in fury. Liuda comes in to try to mollify him: 'Try the jam.' Distracted only momentarily, he despatches her back to the kitchen: 'Go on, the jam will burn.' 'Is it true?' he asks Volodia, and again Liuda listens from behind the gauze while her fate is debated by the men. 'It's true. If you like, I'll move out. After all, I'm here without the right to living space.'

In a crucial intervention into her own life, Liuda draws back the curtain and announces: 'Volodia stays!' His masculine pride routed, Kolia puts on his scarf and cap: 'In that case ... I'm leaving ... you two live together [zhivite vdvoem]'. He leaves the flat, as both Volodia and Liuda look away in embarrassment.

We next see Kolia 'At work outside work hours' (something he had bluntly refused to countenance at the start of the film). In a sardonic parody of the theory of multi-functional furniture he attempts to sleep on a desk. He makes a pillow from a pile of papers; but his feet stick off the edge and his jacket does not cover him. He dreams of home comforts: he sees himself swinging in a rocking chair; stretched out on the bed; stroking the cat; stroking Liuda's arm; and having a cigarette – the hierarchy of these pleasures is an eloquent measure of his domestic priorities. 'I'm a builder myself, but I've got nowhere to live', he mutters.

A morning scene of Volodia and Liuda in bed, facing away from each other, directly quotes the scene of Kolia and Liuda at the start of the film. New scenes from Kolia's workplace at the top of the Bolshoi precede an intertitle that tells us that 'The rains had begun'. Liuda is alone as usual, sitting dejectedly at her station at the window, when Kolia calls in for his things. This time he packs for himself. Seemingly crushed, he makes no appeal. He goes back out into the rain, and the wind of the outside world again gets into the flat, blowing the newspapers off the table. Once more Liuda takes a step – she darts out into the rain *on her own* and brings Kolia back: 'After all, you've got nowhere to go, and the sofa is free anyway.' It seems that the hierarchy of spatial relations in the flat has been fundamentally overturned: first Kolia hands the sofa to Volodia without consulting his wife; then Liuda decides that Volodia will stay; now she allots the sofa to Kolia.

Volodia and Kolia

'The three of them together again' [Opiat' vtroem], says an intertitle, and after a shot of the cat, the fourth member of the household, 'What will happen next?' This is the only intertitle in the film to address the viewer with a question, which underlines the significance of the following scene. The 'answer' to the question is that, in an ironic twist of the theme of domestic contentment, the camera moves to show Kolia and Volodia absorbed in a game of draughts, while Liuda sits bored at her window.[135]

In Pushkin's poem 'It's Winter. What can we do in the country?', draughts was an activity for a monotonous country evening.[136] In Boris Barnet's film *Outskirts* [Okraina, 1933], which begins in 1914, it is a sign of provincial backwardness. Near the start of the film, Greshin, the owners of the cobblers' workshop, and his German friend Robert Karlovich, both of them men of extremely conservative views, sit playing draughts; at the end, just after news reaches the town of the storming of the Winter Palace, Greshin's daughter Manka refuses to play a game with her father and casts the board to the ground.

There is a game of draughts at the Komsomol club in Fridrikh Ermler's *The Parisian Cobbler* [Parizhskii sapozhnik, 1928], and draughts and chess are played in the Workers' Club in *The Man with the Movie Camera*,[137] but the ideological implications of chess are very different. According to Krupskaia it was Lenin's favourite game, and he became honorary president of the Moscow Chess Society in November 1922.[138] In the words of Walter Benjamin, 'Thanks to Lenin, who himself was a chess player, chess has been officially sanctioned in Russia', and he noted the profusion of chess tables in the Red Army Club.[139] The function of chess as an instrument of male bonding (and female exclusion) is played upon in the charming comedy *Chess Fever* [Shakhmatnaia goriachka, 1925] which Vsevolod Pudovkin directed with Nikolai Shpikovsky. The film is set during a world tournament that took place in Moscow in November 1925, and a fascination with the game is seen to unite males across all boundaries of age, race or social station. The obsession of the hero, also played by Vladimir Fogel, is such that all his clothes are made in chessboard patterns, and that he actually forgets to turn up for his own wedding. Thus, as in this scene in *Bed and Sofa*, Fogel's character is torn between love of the game and love of a woman. *Chess Fever* is a comedy, and has a happy ending. The hero's fiancée, frustrated at every turn, herself discovers an enthusiasm for the game, and, in a punning double entendre, suggests they try the Sicilian defence. The hero's two loves can be combined. But Room, in his pre-film statement, had not offered to answer the questions he posed, and the tensions of *Bed and Sofa* are not so easily resolved.

Liuda, dazzled out of her reverie by the headlights of a passing vehicle, goes and stands over the game. But the men are still absorbed. Kolia has Volodia on the ropes. 'I-have-lo-ock-ed-you-in', he sings, and boyishly mimes incarceration. Liuda prepares for bed.

Kolia asks if Volodia wants a cup of tea. Tea drinking as an emblem of *byt* is an image widely used by Mayakovsky, whose imagery pervades *Bed and Sofa*. In the play *Vladimir Mayakovsky. A Tragedy* his soul, dressed in a pale blue dressing-gown, offers him a little glass of tea to soothe his mad sorrow, and his mother makes the same kind offer in *About That*, leading him to exclaim 'Is that it? / You're substituting tea for love? / You're substituting darning socks for love?'[140]

As Liuda takes off her blouse, Kolia modestly averts his gaze. Volodia ostentatiously fails to do so, reminding Kolia that he is the present sexual proprietor, though Kolia eventually shames him into doing so. All of this is seen by Liuda – throughout the film Giber uses snatched glances with extraordinary delicacy to suggest the nuances of the unfolding relationships. Volodia despatches Kolia to the kitchen and repeats the phrase to himself – 'Right, now we'll have some tea' – but the look on his face and the intercut shot of Liuda lying on the bed invest the words with ambiguity.

In the kitchen Kolia is having difficulty with the unfamiliar task of lighting the primus stove. Volodia offers to take over and despatches

12. Volodia and Kolia play draughts

Kolia for loaves. As they talk, Liuda's photo is visible on the wall between them and they form a triangle: Knave, Queen, King. Volodia's deviousness is revealed as he lights the stove with ease. Outside in the street the lamplighter lights the lamp, reversing his action at the beginning of the film. Kolia rushes happily back with four little loaves, two for each of them … only to see the kettle steaming symbolically in the empty kitchen and Volodia's shirt hanging over the screen that hides the bed. Enraged, he lies down on the sofa and covers his head in a pillow. Sexual desire has trumped male comradeship – for now.

The next intertitle, 'And every evening' [I kazhdyi vecher], reveals that the men are still playing draughts, but torpidly, without any of their earlier enthusiasm. At the start of the film time had seemed a neutral, dependable progression of days, ritually registered by the removal of a page from the calendar. In Kolia's absence, passion had made time stand still. Now it has become dully, oppressively repetitive. The phrase 'And every evening' is taken from one of the most famous Russian poems of the early twentieth century, Alexander Blok's lament of urban ennui 'The Unknown Woman' [Neznakomka, 1906]. Every evening [I kazhdyi vecher (the phrase is used recurrently)] the poem's protagonist sits dully drinking in a crowded bar. And every evening a young woman enters the bar and 'takes up her place at the window'. The hero gazes at the young woman and is drawn into a lost world of charm and innocence. At the end of the poem the vision is attributed to the wine he has been drinking, but, at least for a time, transcendence had seemed possible.[141] In this scene in *Bed and Sofa* Liuda too is at her station, looking out of the open window, but Kolia and Volodia pay her no attention at all.

Liuda decides to make a move. She puts on her hat and comes over to the game. She suggests to Volodia that they go for a walk. He seems to accept, but then is dissuaded by Kolia. There is a shot of her back as she stands between them: King, Queen, Knave. Next she tries to persuade Kolia, but now Volodia summons him back to finish the game. 'I'm fed up with both of you' [Nadoeli vy oba], she says, linking them directly for the first time. But still she is not ready to go out for a walk alone – she returns to the window and gazes out, still wearing her hat.

In the eloquent words of Carol Pateman, 'To explore the subjection of women is also to explore the fraternity of men.'[142] Liuda may once have been able to 'lure' Kolia from the game, but over the long haul (and sportsmen continually remind us after a setback that it is the long haul that counts) the safe, predictable comradeship of the two men asserts its power. In her excellent study of *Bed and Sofa* Judith Mayne traces the roots of this comradeship back to the first scenes after Volodia moves into the flat. Even at this stage, the security of their shared military past leads Kolia to spend more time with – and to show more uncomplicated affection for – Volodia, than for his wife. As the film progresses it becomes more and more apparent that 'Kolya and Volodya might be the real couple in *Bed and Sofa*'.[143] In her analysis Mayne deploys a term first used by the critic Eve Kosofsky Sedgwick, 'male homosocial desire'.

In her book *Between Men: English Literature and Male Homosocial Desire*, Kosofsky Sedgwick in turn reports the conclusions of the French critic René Girard about the rivalry between the two active members of fictional erotic triangles. Girard insists that: 'in any erotic rivalry, the bond that links the two rivals is as intense and potent as the bond that links either of the rivals to the beloved: [...] the bonds of "rivalry" and "love", differently as they are experienced, are equally powerful and in many senses equivalent.'[144] Kosofsky Sedgwick herself further stresses that 'the status of women, and the whole question of arrangements between genders, is deeply and inescapably inscribed in the structure even of relationships that seem to exclude women – even in male homosocial/homosexual relationships', and that, 'in any male-dominated society, there is a special relationship between male homosocial (and homosexual) desire and the structures for maintaining and transmitting patriarchal power'.[145]

In a recent overheated study of *Bed and Sofa*, Neya Zorkaya has attempted to read the relationship between Kolia and Volodia as a homosexual one.[146] Application of the term 'homosociality' would seem to offer a considerably subtler and more rewarding approach. Both of the men are clearly erotically drawn to Liuda. Yet both of them also seem incapable of the sustained energy and commitment that this erotic relationship requires. Engaging with Liuda, consulting her and accommodating *her* desires, is too exhausting; how much easier it is for them to exclude and ignore her, and to fill their days with unthreatening, habitual activity.

An unwillingness, or incapacity, to make a sustained commitment to passion causes Oblomov, the preternaturally indolent hero of Ivan Goncharov's novel, to break off his engagement with Olga. In this sense Kolia and Volodia, 'new Soviet men', are following in the footsteps of the embodiment of old Russian torpor. But the conflicting pull of eros and safe male comradeship, most frequently expressed through a shared enthusiasm for sport, is a quintessential masculine dilemma. A highly successful recent English play, *An Evening with Gary Lineker*, set in a Majorcan hotel room on the evening of 4 July 1990, the day of England's World Cup semi-final football match against West Germany, gives a modern reworking of the topos. Monica, who loathes football, is desperate to discuss her strained relationships with Bill, her husband, and Dan, her lover, but nothing can divert them from a live television broadcast of the match. Monica retreats regularly to the balcony, looks out wistfully into the distance and channels her frustration into dreams of her own tryst with Lineker (the star English forward of his generation). Exasperated, she tells Dan, 'It's so sad. You and Bill are exactly the same.'[147]

Liuda and Kolia

An intertitle announces that 'With every day, their life was becoming more difficult'. Liuda is at the window, as usual, while Volodia sits on the sofa in his headphones, listening to the radio. 'Put on the tea', he tells her, and when she fails to do so, he gets up and asks her, 'What is it, are you waiting for him?' When she again refuses to make him tea, he pours himself a glass of sugared water.

Liuda sees feet passing by the window. She puts on her hat and scarf and is about to leave the flat on her own, but Volodia locks her in. 'You're not going anywhere', he tells her, and hides the key in his pocket. Then he returns to his sofa and his radio. When he again refuses to unlock the door, she berates him, 'Husband!' [Muzh!] This is the third time the word has been used in the film, but the first time it has been applied to Volodia, whose relationship with Liuda has deteriorated far faster than did Kolia's. Though Kolia, too, had confined her in this space, he had never actually locked her in; what was metaphorically expressed through Kolia's behaviour is made concrete by Volodia.[148] Again he lies on the sofa, his face to the wall, while Liuda lies on the bed, looking away from him. As the film progresses these eloquent shots of the characters' backs recur ever more frequently.

The clock shows 8.45. Kolia comes back from work and tries the door handle. Volodia sees this, but stuffs the key under his pillow. So Kolia is forced to climb in through the window, and, since Volodia is back on the sofa, he has to sleep in the rocking chair, the third space in the room's triangle.

Liuda wakes in the middle of the night and, feeling sympathy for him, she makes him the tea that she had refused to make Volodia. In contrast to his behaviour at the start of film, Kolia makes no complaint about the drink he is offered. Instead, he rocks contentedly on the rocking chair, as he had done in his dream of home. He smiles, he drums his fingers contentedly … Things are looking up … But Volodia seems to stir on the sofa … Liuda makes the bed, plumping its many bolsters … Volodia awakes and a cat and mouse game ensues between the two men.

In the morning, when the cat wakes Volodia, it is Kolia's clothes he sees hanging over the dividing screen. So Volodia gets up, and finds himself a pillow.[149] Then he turns to the wall and puts the pillow over his head to drown out what he cannot bear to think about. Not for the first time, a pattern of visual and episodic echoes gives rhythm to the film and seamlessly advances the plot.

Liuda, Volodia and Kolia: *Ménage à Trois*

From this point on the trio live together in a version of the relationship made famous by Chernyshevsky. Aleksandra Kollontai, in her 1923 article 'Make Way for the Winged Eros' (discussed above), had condoned a simultaneous attraction to two members of the opposite sex. Iuri Olesha would parody the idea in his *Envy*, written between February and June 1927, at the time when *Bed and Sofa* was showing in Moscow. At the novel's end the heroes Kavalerov and Ivan Babichev, disillusioned and reduced to a cynical cult of indifference, take turns to sleep in the ghastly bed of the hideous widow Anechka.[150] Chernyshevsky himself, in *What is to be Done?*, had presented an idealised version of triangular relations by making sure that they did not actually take place. What is most eloquent about the treatment of the subject in *Bed and Sofa* is that the film contains no scenes of any successful living together. Instead, immediately after Volodia puts the pillow over his head, an intertitle announces that 'Two months have passed', leading us directly to the final crisis in the trio's shared life.

In this climactic scene the three of them are, once again, isolated in their proximity. In her 1918 speech 'The Family and the Communist State', Kollontai had described the new form of marriage as a 'free [...] union' in which 'there is no more domestic slavery for women!'[151] Here Liuda, in a headscarf and with her sleeves rolled up like the household drudge, is doing the washing in a heavy iron tub. Volodia is also in the kitchen, intent on his cooking. Kolia, in the main room, is busy with his technical drawings. Suddenly Liuda faints. When Volodia questions her she nods affirmatively. Volodia comes into the main room, slumps at the table, and says to Kolia: 'You know – Liuda is pregnant.' It is further evidence of her move towards autonomy that Liuda has not told the men of her situation. Kolia goes into the kitchen to check whether it is true ...

Pregnancy

Maternity provisions were increased after the Revolution, in part in order to accommodate women into the labour force. Paid maternity leave, first introduced in December 1917, was formalised in the 1918 Labour Code.[152] The official position at the time of Liuda's pregnancy was outlined in N. V. Shchepkin's *The Protection of Mother and Child According to Our Laws. A Short Reference Guide for Mothers*, issued by the publishing house of the Department for the Protection of Motherhood and Infancy [Okhrana materinstva i mladenchestva] in 1927. The guide's introduction stressed the Soviet state's concern for the rights of mothers and children, which were given legal expression. The guide itself consisted of forty points, of which points 3 to 11 covered pregnancy. Point 8, covering the duties of fathers, began: 'The father of a child is required to contribute to the expenses involved in the pregnancy, the birth, and the upkeep of the mother of the child throughout pregnancy and for six months after the birth.' (What was to happen then is not indicated.) If a father refused to contribute, he could be pursued by the courts. If paternity had to be established by the court, then 'the father of the child is the man indicated by the mother', and 'he will be required to contribute to expenses'.[153]

Needless to say, reality was not always as dictated by the law. Women members of the Komsomol found that pregnancy led to mockery and exclusion.[154] The motif of a man's abandonment of a pregnant woman is also widespread in the films of the time.

In Alexander Dovzhenko's first film, *Love's Little Berry* [Iagodka liubvi, 1926], man's sexual and social irresponsibility is presented in comic form. The vain and stupid hero, the barber Zhan Kolbasiuk (Jean Saucisson), is presented by his girlfriend Liza with 'their child'. Since he is not prepared to care for it, he tries to palm it off on a number of other men from a range of ages and social classes. Each without exception also deploys ruses to get rid of it and each time he gets it back.[155] Meanwhile Liza goes to a People's Court and Jean gets a summons to appear and to pay for the child's upbringing. Terrified by the threatening features of the People's Investigator, he decides to marry the girl and become a model father. In the final scene of family happiness he asks, 'Liza! Is our baby a boy or a girl?', to which she replies, 'It was my aunt's child'. Dovzhenko's hero may be irresponsible, but he is also preternaturally stupid, while his heroine deploys deviousness to hook her man.

The question is also addressed in two films of the period by Fridrikh Ermler. The first, co-directed with Eduard Ioganson, is *Katka the Reinette Apple Seller* [Kat′ka, Bumazhnyi ranet, 1926], which opened in December 1926, three months before *Bed and Sofa*. Katka has come from her village to Leningrad and works as an unlicensed street trader, selling the apples of the title. She gets pregnant by a local hoodlum, Semka Zhgut (Valeri Solovtsov, who looks startlingly like the young Robert de Niro). But he is also involved with NEP good-time girl Verka, who trades in phoney Chypre and Coty perfume ('only without the stoppers'). Realising that Semka is no good, Katka leaves him. She meets the excessively timid Vadka, an intellectual fallen on hard times. Thus two triangles are formed in the film. One places a good woman (Katka) between good and bad men; the other puts a bad man (Semka) between good and bad women. By the end of the film they have resolved themselves into two couples, a good one and a bad one. The bad pair fall further and further into NEP low life and criminality and at the end of the film they are arrested. The good pair go through several trials, but virtue is rewarded. The film is particularly remarkable for its reversal of conventional sexual roles. Vadka stays at home and looks after the baby, which is not his, changes her nappies, does the ironing. When he tries to get a job selling apples, he proves to be hopeless at it. Several times Semka comes round to try to take his baby, and each time he terrorises a cowering Vadka. It is Katka who has to come back and beat Semka up – as she has previously beaten up Verka. Despairing, Vadka tries to commit suicide. He botches even that, but his 'resurrection' changes him, and at the end of the film, he does stand up to Semka. Nevertheless, it is Katka who goes out and gets work at a factory, leaving Vadka to look after the child. At the end of the film, as the two of them look into the camera in turn and their daughter gurgles happily, we witness the creation of an unconventional Soviet family.[156]

In 1927, Ermler used the same actors to make a variation on the theme, this time set in the world of the Komsomol, *The Parisian Cobbler* [Parizhskii sapozhnik].[157] Both the heroine, Katia, and her boyfriend, Andrei, are Komsomol members, and they work in a paper factory in a provincial town. Kirik Rudenko, the deaf and dumb cobbler of the title, is also secretly in love with Katia. When Katia finds that she is pregnant, Andrei is furious, but tells her he will think of something. He asks Grisha, the secretary of their Komsomol cell, for advice. Grisha searches distractedly in his papers, finds a book with 'Sexual Problems' on the spine, and gives it to him. Looking at the cover Andrei sees the full title is *Sexual Problems in Russian Prose Fiction*, and throws it away in disgust. Instead he turns for help to the local hooligan, Motka, and his friends. Motka tells him that if Katia has sexual relations with all the group, she will lose the child. Andrei arranges for Katia to go late at night to a secluded area where the hooligans are lying in wait. They set upon her, but she manages to escape. All of this is witnessed by the lovelorn Kirik. To cover their wounded pride the hooligans tell Andrei that they have done the deed. Rumours about Katia spread through the town, but Kirik manages both to explain to the Komsomol members what really happened and to save Katia from a furious Motka. Andrei is dismissed from the Komsomol. Once again the good man is the man who is weak and initially marginalised.

It is remarkable in the context of *Bed and Sofa* how often Andrei presents his odious actions as an attack on *meshchanstvo*, petit-bourgeois philistinism. Turning to Motka for help he says: 'I now have a mass of problems on grounds of *meshchanstvo*. If I start smelling of nappies, I'll lose all my authority' (in the factory, where he has a responsible job). When he tells Katia that he has found a solution, he adds 'just don't be bourgeois about it' [tol´ko bez meshchanstva]. Back in his parents' *petit-bourgeois* interior with its potted plants and caged bird, he reads the paper at meal time (as Volodia does in *Bed and Sofa*). When his enraged father tears the paper away from him, saying, 'Don't dare to read the paper at table in my house!', he tells him, 'You are an alien-to-modernity individual. Dad – you're a petit bourgeois!' [Papasha! Vy – meshchanin!]) And the note he gets the hooligans to give Katia reads: 'Katiushenka, leave *meshchanstvo* behind and believe me. I have learnt that if you go with a number of people your pregnancy will be liquidated. Trust the lads. To the grave, Andrei.' The heavy irony of this device makes it transparent whose behaviour the film-makers really consider to be philistine. At the end of the film the angry eyes of a young woman look straight to camera and the classic Russian question 'Who is Guilty?' [Kto vinovat?] appears as the film's last intertitle. Yet, for all this, the analysis of the problem provided by *The Parisian Cobbler* is primitive.

Both of Ermler's films are heavily propagandistic, with a clear delineation between good and bad characters and moral anxiety worn on the sleeve. In this sense they differ fundamentally from *Bed and Sofa* which, despite its title, never introduces discussions of *meshchanstvo* into its dialogue and merely hints at it in Liuda's final letter.

Like the seemingly weak and ineffectual Vadka in *Katka the Reinette Apple Seller*, Andrei, the fireman hero of Evgeni Cherviakov's *My Son* [Moi syn, 1928], discovers the moral resources to take on another man's child. Early in the film his wife Olga confesses that the child she has just given birth to is not his. The rumours swirling around the communal flat they live in play on his nerves and he makes frequent scenes. In despair, Olga leaves him and gets a job as a pointswoman. Andrei's comrades accuse him of bourgeois prejudice. One day, the house Olga is living in burns down. He risks his life to save the child and his bravery brings about their reconciliation. He becomes a model father to the boy.[158]

If the didactic intent of *Katka the Reinette Apple Seller* and *My Son* is transparent, neither protagonist in *Bed and Sofa* is capable of such self-sacrifice. While Volodia counts back the weeks against a calendar, Kolia tells Liuda: 'You must have an abortion. I do not want to have another man's child.' He returns and says the same thing to Volodia: 'Liuda must have an abortion ... we ... ', but his words are interrupted by Liuda, back at her curtained way-station between the kitchen and the main room. 'Going halves on an abortion,' she says with disgust. 'What were you both [oba] thinking about earlier?' For the second time she uses the word that links them. The trio are plunged into silence and Liuda looks away in anguish.

Abortion?

On 18 November 1920 a common decree of the Commissariats of Justice and Health had legalised free abortion in the country. The operation was to take place only in hospitals and to be performed by doctors. It was recognised as a social necessity rather than as a woman's right. Peasants and other midwives performing abortions would continue to be prosecuted. A 1924 film *Abortion* [Abort], directed by G. Lemberg and N. Baklin, made as part of the propaganda campaign against illegal abortions, combined medical information with a fictional story. After the death of a woman who has undergone a botched illegal abortion, the midwife responsible is arrested and found guilty by the court.

In January 1924 the Commissariat of Health instructed local sections of the Department for the Protection of Motherhood and Infancy to set up commissions to interview women who wanted abortions. Women with medical problems and the families of workers were given priority for free hospital abortions, but unemployed married women were at the bottom of the list. Legal abortion was considerably more widespread in the towns, and in 1926 39 per cent of the hospital abortions were performed in Moscow and Leningrad. The main reasons women cited for wanting an abortion were poverty, housing conditions and illness.

By the late 1920s there was widespread concern about the falling birth-rate. From the end of the decade there was a powerful anti-abortion campaign, and payment for the operation was introduced. Abortion was banned in the Soviet Union in 1936. A joint resolution of the Central Executive Committee and the Soviet of People's Commissars of the USSR was published on the front page of *Pravda* on 26 May 1936, then issued as pamphlet. It passed into law a month later. Abortion would remain illegal until 1955.[159]

The official attitude to abortion at the time of the making of *Bed and Sofa* is made clear in the relevant section of *The Protection of Mother and Child According to our Laws*:

> According to our laws, a woman who has an abortion is not punished. But if the state does not punish abortion, that is not because it encourages or approves of it, but only because you cannot bring down the number of abortions by penal measures. Instead of punishing women, the state takes their interests and health under its protection. Therefore abortion is permitted only with the agreement of the pregnant woman herself. The operation must be carried out in hospital conditions, and only by people with special medical training, that is to say doctors […] Abortions can take place in Soviet hospitals and also in private clinics.[160]

„Bett und Sofa"

13. The abortion clinic. Liuda is seated on the far right

It is to a private clinic that Liuda goes in *Bed and Sofa*. We see her sitting fiddling nervously with a card with the number five on it – she is fifth in the queue. She sees a woman undressing behind a screen and changing into a white dressing-gown. A number of other women are sitting in the clinic. A well-dressed young woman is being calmed by her mother. A solemn woman in a shawl (perhaps already the mother of several children) sits quietly on her own. There is another group of two women, the older one cajoling the younger. Liuda looks around the room. Through the range of social types, Room hints at the different reasons which would bring women to the abortion clinic and provides parallels for Liuda's fate.

A nurse emerges, and a second nurse bows to a white-coated doctor as he emerges from the operating room. The doctor walks through the waiting room turning up his sleeves and the women nod deferentially to him. We see a NEP flapper type in high heels, sitting smoking. The nurse calls out, 'Third': the woman in the dressing-gown goes into the operating room and Liuda shudders; 'Fourth': Liuda checks her card, and the woman in the shawl goes in.

It turns out that Liuda is sitting by a window; she pushes it open to get some air. Looking out she sees a young boy nursing a doll. She smiles. In contrast with the recurrent scenes in the flat, this time Liuda looks *down*, and for the first time in the film the scene that she sees in the outside world is complete and in focus. Looking out for a second time she sees a baby swaddled in lace, and smiles again at this pretty vision before being thrown into further anxiety. Suddenly there is a panic in the operating room. The nurse rushes out and summons her colleague. The young woman with her mother faints. Liuda mechanically tears up her card. The doctor again emerges from the operating room.

'Your turn', says the mother of the young woman, and the nurse calls out 'Fifth', but Liuda rushes from the clinic. The nurse goes over and shuts the window. What she sees outside is far less idyllic: two young children are lying in a pram and one has an empty container in his hand – two more mouths to feed.[161] The nurse calls 'Next', and in goes the flapper, taking a last drag from her cigarette, smoothing her hair and adjusting her clothes.

The scene in the abortion clinic contains a number of eloquent echoes of life in the flat on Third Meshchanskaia Street. A woman undresses and drapes her clothes over a screen. Liuda sits by the window, alone with her thoughts. Breathlessly, she throws open the window in search of solace. Most notably of all, the clinic, like the flat, is a place where a man presides over women. In the health propaganda posters of the 1920s Soviet medicine was represented by a male doctor in a white coat, assisted by female nurses, despite the fact that there were already many women in the profession.[162] Here, too, a male doctor is assisted by two female nurses, and fawned upon by his female patients. And in a bizarre and unsettling extension of this male principle, the officious nurse addresses the women as *masculine* numbers, calling out *Tretii, Chetvertyi, Piatyi* [Third number, Fourth, Fifth], and finally *Sleduiushchii* [Next]. So the metaphors of suffocation and oppression in the flat are made concrete in the clinic.

In one script variant Liuda did, in fact, go through with the abortion as a prelude to leaving the men.[163] This was discarded in favour of a more open ending, but the final version of the scene in the clinic contains elements of melodrama – the unseen panic in the operating room – and of didacticism – the insouciance of the NEP flapper type – that are not present in the rest of the film. This has led some critics to suggest that Shklovsky and Room were influenced by the increasingly vocal pro-maternity campaign of the period.[164] Others, however, find Liuda's decision a logical extension of the role she has already taken on. Molly Haskell suggests that she has long since been behaving as a 'mother' to the two men, who have reverted to 'infancy', and that in this context her change of mind, 'a reversal that has been viewed as a palliative to producers, [...] can be viewed more charitably as an understandable change of heart'. For Haskell, Liuda's is a 'lonely moral triumph, [...] preferring the one baby in her belly to the two grown ones left behind'.[165]

Leaving and Staying: Liuda

Liuda returns to the flat and prepares to leave. Some critics argued, both on the film's release and later, that she should have stayed, taken the alimony allowed her by the 1926 Family Code, and forced the men out of the flat.[166] In practice, as Wendy Goldman has pointed out, this was not always easily achieved. Divorced women faced a range of problems, including unemployment, a lack of crèches, difficulties in getting alimony and limitations on the time for which it could be claimed. The courts worked very slowly, and when defendants refused to pay, punitive measures were rarely applied.[167]

The theme of single motherhood became widespread in the art of the time. At the end of *Vasilisa Malygina*, Kollontai's heroine, realising that she is pregnant, determines not to return to her ghastly husband. When her doctor asks how she will manage 'all on your own with a child', she replies, 'But I won't be alone', for she intends to set up a crèche at the textile factory where she works:

> She walked back along the street, smiling. A baby! How wonderful! She'd be a model mother! After all, it should be possible to bring up a child in true communist fashion. There was no reason for women to set up with husbands, in families if it merely tied them to the cooking and the domestic chores. They'd get a crèche going, and re-purchase a children's hostel. It would be a demonstration of child-rearing to everyone.[168]

Thus Vasilisa puts into practice the ideas Kollontai propagandised in her speeches and articles.

An even more radical stance is taken by Milda, the Latvian communist heroine of Sergei Tretiakov's play *I Want a Child!* [Khochu rebenka, 1926]. All Milda's choices about her personal life are rational and matter-of-fact. Deciding that she wants a child, and certain that its father must be 100 per cent proletarian, she chooses Iakov, who already has a de facto wife, Lipa, but who is the pride of the factory sports team. Informing him of her intentions she compares reproduction to factory production and adds: 'I don't want a husband. I want a child. It's not you that I need. It's your sperm that I need.' After she becomes pregnant she sidelines Iakov, insisting that she will bring up the child not with the help of a man but with the help of the state, sending it to the factory nursery, which, conveniently, has just been completed.

In a deeply compromised final scene, set in 1930, four years into the utopian future, Iakov, Milda and Lipa form a happy model triangle. Both Milda and Lipa have two children and they share top prize at a baby show.[169]

In September 1926, Tretiakov signed an agreement with Meyerhold for the production of his play, and Meyerhold's preparations coincided with the filming of *Bed and Sofa*. He described the production in the Moscow newspaper *Vecherniaia Moskva* on 2 November 1926 as 'on the subject of sex and marriage in the conditions of the new *byt*'.[170] Production of the play was banned in 1927, though efforts continued to get it staged. At a meeting of Glavrepertkom, the theatre censorship committee, on 4 December 1928, Room spoke passionately in its support: 'Banning this piece in the theatre and the cinema will cause despondency among film directors. We should eliminate lisping [siusiukan´e] with the viewer.'[171] He had used the same word [podsiusiukivanie] in the statement he gave in 1926 in defence of the stance of *Bed and Sofa* [see the translation of this statement, pp. 11–13], and in the late 1920s he attempted to film Tretiakov's play, but the plan did not come to fruition.[172]

Single parenthood was also addressed in a number of contemporary films. Oleg Frelikh's *Prostitute* [Prostitutka, 1926] was released on 15 March 1927, the same day as *Bed and Sofa*. It tells the story of Nadezhda, who lives contentedly in Moscow, with her market trader husband and her children. When their neighbour Liuba is tricked into prostitution, Nadezhda is disapproving. After her husband dies in an accident, however, she is reduced to destitution, and when her children fall ill, she herself contemplates the same fate. At her lowest point she even attempts suicide. But Frelikh's heavily didactic film – which includes an illustrated lecture on the causes and the social consequences of prostitution – is eager to show how the state can help the unfortunate: through the intervention of a woman doctor Liuba gets a job in a sewing workshop (echoing the experience of the women helped by Vera Pavlovna in *What is to be Done?*). Through this she meets a Komsomol member, Shura, and he arranges for Nadezhda to work as a pointswoman on the trams. At the end of the film Nadezhda visits her young daughter, happily ensconced in a state orphanage.

In Mikhail Doronin's *The Wife* [Zhena, 1927] made at the same studio as *Bed and Sofa* and released seven months after it, Glazkov, the assistant director of a textile factory, though a great orator on Soviet morality at public meetings, is very patriarchal at home. When he takes up with a dancer, his wife, Varvara, succumbs to the advances of Anton, the chairman of the factory committee, played by Nikolai Batalov. When he too turns out to be a scoundrel, Varvara leaves both men, takes her children and herself gets work in a textile factory.

A variation on the theme is provided in *The Circle* [Krug, 1927], directed by Iuli Raizman and Alexander Gavronsky. The hero, Bersenev, an assistant prosecutor, is too busy to pay much attention to his wife, Vera, who feels oppressed by the life of a domestic lapdog. She is seduced by Poliansky, a NEP playboy. When he comes before Bersenev's court for stealing state property, it turns out that Vera is his accomplice. Bersenev lets the law take its course, takes their child and parts from his wife for ever.

In all the treatments of single parenthood discussed here, the parent is not required to bring up the child on his or her own, but relies upon the state network of nurseries and crèches and is thoroughly integrated into the Soviet employment system. Liuda's position in *Bed and Sofa* is crucially different. She has not planned her pregnancy like Tretiakov's Milda. She is not supported by a circle of friends like Vasilisa Malygina. She is not, like them, a member of the Party. She has no job and cannot take advantage of factory child-care facilities.

She makes no application to the 'Houses of Mother and Child' or the 'Working Hostels' for unemployed women outlined in Shchepkin's guide.[173] Here, as earlier, what is most eloquent about Room and Shklovsky's script is its silences. Liuda is, and remains, completely outside the official Soviet system, and by this stance she calls its efficacy into question.

In the flat on Third Meshchanskaia Street, Liuda packs, this time for herself, not her husband. She takes her photograph from the wall, and when it will not fit into her case she removes it from its frame, symbolically replacing the empty frame on the wall. She looks at herself in the mirror, which is surrounded by trinkets. She sheds a tear on a plaster cat inscribed, 'To Liudochka, in fond remembrance', and stuffs it into her case. Then she writes a simple note: 'I'm leaving ... I shall never return to your [vashu] Meshchanskaia [Street].' Again she links the two men, and this time she links them to the *meshchanstvo* which the film excoriates, while writing herself out of the space of the flat and explicitly assigning it to them. In an earlier version of the note she had told them: 'I've taken some books. I want to study. To work at a trade myself.'[174] Now she merely mutters to herself in reassurance: 'It's all right ... I'll work ... I'll survive.' What remains clear is her determination to live her own life. In *What is to be Done?* Vera Pavlovna had concluded 'There is no real happiness without total independence. Poor women! There are so few of you who experience this happiness.'[175] Women's independence had also recently received radical new support from Kollontai. In a 1926 article entitled 'Marriage, Women and Alimony', she had attacked alimony as the continuation of women's subjection and proposed instead the institution of a general insurance fund, which would guarantee support to single mothers and their children. It is particularly noteworthy that the article appeared, with a portrait of Kollontai, on the cover of the film magazine *Ekran*. Given Liuda's enthusiasm for the cinema, we might fancifully suggest that it influenced her decision.[176]

Meanwhile, Kolia and Volodia arrive at the abortion clinic. They are late and it has already closed. They take off their hats in unison and ask, 'Is Semenova here?' The nurse looks distrustfully from the one to the other and says, 'Who's asking?' They look at each other and reply in turn, 'The husband' [Muzh], applying to themselves the word which Liuda had used of them when they treated her especially

14. Liuda prepares to leave the flat for ever

badly.[177] The nurse looks quizzical; she checks her notes. 'Semenova left … she got scared.' In unison the men put on their caps and leave. The nurse shuts the door.

Back at the flat, Liuda gives the yardman her papers and insists, despite his protests, that he deregister her from this 'living space'.

She wipes away her tears. He gives her back the amended papers, doffs his cap and wishes her good luck. They shake hands ... there is a shot of a tram in motion ... the yardman spits, curses, and pulls the curtain across the door. We see a shot of the Yaroslavl station. Trains from this station go north, but Liuda has chosen it for no other reason than that it is the closest to Third Meshchanskaia Street, one of three stations in a nearby square. Protazanov's *Aelita* had ended with the model couple of soldier (played by Nikolai Batalov) and nurse arriving at a station to embark upon an exemplary journey to help in the reconstruction of the country; later, the journey, ordered by the Party, to tame and educate the periphery, would become a commonplace in Soviet art. In *Bed and Sofa* both Volodia and Kolia had also made journeys to a clear ideological destination. In crucial contrast, no one sanctions Liuda's journey, and neither she nor the viewer has any idea where her journey will end.

Leaving and Staying: Kolia and Volodia

Back in the flat, Kolia sees the cupboard drawers hanging open and the note under the inkwell on the neatly laid table. He reads it and notices that Liuda's photo is missing from the picture frame. Then Volodia reads the note. He takes off his hat. The two men look at each other, their faces reflected in the mirror. Volodia says: 'Kolia, it seems that you and I' – again they look at each other – 'are scoundrels [podletsy].' Kolia looks in the mirror and looks down ...

We cut to the train. Liuda is at a window, though this time the window is in motion. Instead of looking at passing feet, she looks out over all of Russia. A stretch of railway track is emerging from under the carriages.

Kolia is lying on the bed, Volodia on the sofa. Both the men and the articles of furniture, initially contrasted, have now become twins. Liuda leaves, Kolia and Volodia stay. The motifs of stagnation and immobility, with their transparent metaphorical implications, have been transferred from the woman, who has emerged into the world, to the men, who have been sucked into the inertia of the flat. These are not evil men – they do not beat their wife, they are not drunkards, they are not crooks, they do not refuse to work, like the protagonists of several novels and stories, plays and films of the period – and yet they are scoundrels. Not that their awareness of this leads to any change in their behaviour: 'Well, Volodia, shall we have some tea?' asks Kolia. 'Is there any jam left, Kolia?' replies Volodia. Once again there is a couple in the flat, mired in comfortable ritual.

The Ending

Liuda continues her journey. The train moves across the screen from left to right and then away into the depth of the frame, reversing Volodia's journey to Moscow at the start of the film. Liuda is looking out of the window. The train crosses a bridge and continues off into the unknown.

This open ending has irked some critics who cite in their support an explanation offered by Viktor Shklovsky in 1930.[178] Stressing the difficulty he had had in writing the ending, Shklovsky continued: 'and I finished it in purely formal terms – with her departure, which, unfortunately, quickly became a bad habit in Soviet cinematography.' But, as Natalia Nusinova has pointed out, this ending is merely the logical conclusion of what has been happening throughout the film. Shklovsky, not for the first time, is resorting to obfuscation.[179]

Room's allusion to Lermontov in his 1926 statement had prepared viewers for an open-ended film, in which the refusal to resolve all the questions it raised would leave them to make up their own minds. The failure to suggest a destination for Liuda's journey is consistent with this intention, but this does not mean that the film-makers themselves are neutral about the actions of their characters. Eric Naiman has recently argued that: 'In the Russia of NEP, political revulsion was becoming unmentionable, while the taboo on sex was weakening in accordance with the dictates of a self-consciously materialistic age. In this environment, talk about sex became a metaphor – and symptom – for thoughts about something else: politics and ideology.'[180]

Naiman refers elsewhere to 'the social significance of personal life and its essential synecdoche: sex',[181] and the overarching subversive ideological implications of Liuda's behaviour are scarcely hidden. At the end of *Bed and Sofa*, the heroine leaves not just the men who have oppressed her, but also the capital city that they inhabit. She abandons the ideological centre of the Soviet state, and takes a journey with no known destination. She thus reverses not only the action of one of the heroes at the start of the film, but also the 'coming to Moscow' motif that became ideologically dominant in Soviet culture in future decades.[182] It is the leaving, not the destination that is important. Liuda rejects not just the 'utopian' *ménage à trois* but also the Socialist male city, which is incapable of acknowledging, let alone addressing, her desires. By her eloquent failure to turn for help to Party, or women's committee, or factory, or any other social network, she condemns them as irrelevant and dismisses the ubiquitous propaganda of the model Soviet society and the new Soviet family. Her departure from Third Meshchanskaia Street, and from Moscow, is a rejection of all Soviet systems. At the same time, she refuses to consider her situation as a tragedy ('It's all right ... . I'll survive'). At the time the Zhenotdel had a recurrent mantra: women should resort to self-initiative [samodeiatel′nost′], make their own revolution and construct their own *byt*.[183] This is what Liuda does. But her 'New World' is not a state-sponsored one.

In a parallel which suggests the extraordinary daring of the film-makers, Liuda's behaviour echoes that of the character of O-90 in Evgeni Zamiatin's anti-utopian novel *We* [My], which, though banned in the Soviet Union, had been published in English in 1924 and was certainly known to Shklovsky. In the One State of *We*, multiple sexual partners are the norm, but sexual relations are strictly controlled and children are brought up centrally by the state. When O-90 becomes illicitly pregnant, she realises that she will be put to death as soon as she has given birth. So she escapes from the One State 'beyond the green wall' to have her baby and live in the free, uncharted beyond. Liuda, too, is 'illicitly' pregnant, and she too evades the order to abort her child by leaving the oppressive city for ever.

Perhaps, too, Liuda felt the need to escape from increasingly conservative social policy and the new model Soviet family. By the 1930s, the utopian vision of the eradication of bourgeois domesticity would be completely abandoned. In 1934 the magazine *Rabotnitsa* [The Woman Worker] published the 'exemplary oath' which the housewife N. Zaitseva had made to her husband:

I promise to create comfort in our apartment, prepare meals on time, keep your work clothes in order, and I require in turn that you do not lose a minute in your shock work and that there are no lapses in your work discipline and that you pass your technical examinations with your worker brigade with the highest marks.[184]

Liuda had already sampled the creation of comfort ('It's Saturday. Don't forget to wash the floors'); the preparation of meals ('You can make us some jam'); and the mending of a torn shirt. She was not excited by worker brigades. Life in the backwoods with her child was, somehow, preferable.

Notes

1. Quoted in R. Taylor and I. Christie (eds), *The Film Factory: Russian and Soviet Cinema in Documents 1896–1939* (London, 1988), p. 128.
2. The statement appeared as '"Tret'ia Meshchanskaia". (Beseda s rez-hisserom A. M. Roomom)', in *Kino*, 14 September 1926, pp. 1–2; it was reprinted in V. Zabrodin (ed.), *Abram Matveevich Room. 1894–1976. Materialy k retrospektive fil'mov* (Moscow, 1994), pp. 13–15, from which it is translated here.
3. Room would always be considered an 'actor's director'. In a 1932 article 'Akter – polpred idei' [The actor is the plenipotentiary of the idea], he would insist: 'The actor is the author of his own creative explication of the image.' Cited in V. Korotkii, '"Tret'ia Meshchanskaia" Abrama Rooma: nekotorye nachala analiza fil'ma. Stat'ia 1', *Tiani-Tolkai*, 1, 1993, pp. 33–60 (p. 60).
4. In his lectures on film-making at the Mezhhrabpomfil'm studio in the autumn of 1929, Shklovskii described *Bed and Sofa* as 'purely plot driven' and contrasted it with 'the approach of montage cinema'; V. Shklovskii, 'Lektsii v "Mezhrabpomfil'me"' [1929], *Kinovedcheskie zapiski*, 41, 1999, pp. 126–60 (p. 136).
5. I have not been able to establish the precise implications of the reference to 'Italian book-keeping' [ital'ianskaia bukhgalteriia], though the double-entry system of book-keeping was instituted with the development of the commercial republics in Italy. Room's insistence upon the creative aesthetic of economy is clearly at the root of the allusion.
6. This was the amount of living space officially allocated to Soviet workers at the time. An arshin is an old Russian measure of length equal to 71 cm.
7. The Sukharev Tower was built in the 1690s on the Garden Ring [Sadovoe kol'tso] in central Moscow on the instructions of Peter the Great. It had a large clock tower and dominated the area. It was dismantled in 1934.
8. In the film as made, the husband works on the reconstruction of the Bolshoi Theatre.
9. Vikt. Iuz, 'Na ocherednye temy. "Problema pola"', *Zhenskii zhurnal*, 2,

1926, p. 4; quoted in Eric Naiman, *Sex in Public. The Incarnation of Early Soviet Ideology* (Princeton, NJ, 1997), p. 107.

10. Naiman, *Sex in Public*, pp. 119, 115, 147. For a brilliant discussion of the debate and its manipulation see ibid., especially chapters 3 and 4.

11. W. Benjamin, *Moscow Diary* (London, 1986), p. 55.

12. M. Iu. Lermontov, 'Geroi nashego vremeni', *Sobranie sochinenii v chetyrekh tomakh* (Moscow–Leningrad, 1958–59), Vol. 4, pp. 276–7. Compare Room's words, 'Dovol'no obkarmlivat' zritelia sladkimi skazkami', with Lermontov's, 'Dovol'no liudei kormili slastiami'.

13. Room's recollection is in his memoir 'Iunost' byvaet odnazhdy. Vspominaet Abram Room', *Iskusstvo kino*, 2, 1974, pp. 15–16. For the *Komsomol'skaia pravda* source, see I. Grashchenkova, *Abram Room* (Moscow, 1977) pp. 85–6.

14. Grashchenkova, *Abram Room*, p. 107.

15. G. Giber, 'Kak snimalas' "Tret'ia Meshchanskaia"', *Sovetskii ekran*, 5, 1927, p. 4.

16. Iutkevich quotes his report for *Sovetskii ekran*, 40, 1926, and adds further details in 'Kak ia stal rezhisserom', in his *Sobranie sochinenii v 3 tomakh* (Moscow, 1990), Vol. 1, pp. 273–333 (pp. 320–4).

17. Grashchenkova, *Abram Room*, pp. 106, 107.

18. This is the figure given by Giber. Room and Shklovsky in pieces written late in life suggest a considerably shorter filming schedule, but Semenova in her memoir of Batalov speaks of a total of two and a half months, consistent with Giber's contemporary report, which I have preferred to trust.

19. Iutkevich, 'Kak ia stal rezhisserom', p. 322; L. Semenova, 'Zhizn' snachala … ', in *Zhizn' v kino. Veterany o sebe i svoikh tovarishchakh*, Vol. 1 (Moscow, 1971), pp. 323–4.

20. Giber, 'Kak snimalas' "Tret'ia Meshchanskaia"'; Room, in an interview with M. Dolinskii, in '"Tret'ia Meshchanskaia". Rasskaz v dokumentakh i odno interv'iu', *Ekran 1968–1969* (Moscow, 1969), pp. 22–4 (p. 23), though this, too, may be an old man's fantasy.

21. Semenova, 'Zhizn' snachala … ', p. 325; *Nikolai Petrovich Batalov. Stat'i, vospominaniia, pis'ma* (Moscow, 1971), p. 164.

22. Both the poster designed by Vladimir and Georgii Stenberg (see Plate 5) and the one designed by Iakov Ruklevskii (Plate 10), each from 1927, style the film '*Liubov' vtroem (Tret'ia Meshchanskaia)*'.

23. Details of these relationships are taken from Irina Paperno's absorbing *Chernyshevsky and the Age of Realism. A Study in the Semiotics of Behavior* (Stanford, CA, 1988). Herzen is discussed on pp. 141–7, Shel'gunov on pp. 147–50.

24. Lopukhov's proposal is in chapter 3, section 25 of the novel, and Rakhmetov's assessment in chapter 3, section 30. Because of the number of existing editions of Chernyshevsky's novel I have considered it more

useful to refer to chapters and sections, rather than to a specific edition. Where, however, I quote directly from the novel, I have used the exemplary translation by Michael R. Katz in N. Chernyshevsky, *What is to be Done?* (Ithaca, NY, and London, 1989).

25. Each of the couples does in fact have a child at the end of the novel, but this information is vouchsafed by Chernyshevsky in passing and the children play no role in the plot. On the 'hostility to progeny' of the religious–utopian tradition in Russia, see Naiman, *Sex in Public*, pp. 27–45. For his reading of *What is to be Done?*, see pp. 36–7.

26. This account is also taken from Paperno, *Chernyshevsky and the Age of Realism*, pp. 138–9.

27. For an account of this and other theorised relationships in Symbolist circles see O. Matich, 'The Symbolist Meaning of Love: Theory and Practice', in I. Paperno and J. Delaney Grossman (eds), *Creating Life. The Aesthetic Utopia of Russian Modernism* (Stanford, CA, 1994), pp. 24–50.

28. On this relationship see A. Pyman, *The Life of Aleksandr Blok. Vol. 1: The Distant Thunder 1880–1908* (Oxford, 1979), especially pp. 236–40.

29. A. Kollontai, 'Dorogu krylatomu erosu', first in *Molodaia gvardiia*, 3, 1923, pp. 111–24; translated as 'Make Way for the Winged Eros' in W. G. Rosenberg (ed.)*Bolshevik Visions. First Phase of the Cultural Revolution in Soviet Russia*, 2nd edn (Ann Arbor, MI, 1990), Part 1, pp. 84–94; quotation on p. 92.

30. 'Three Generations' was first published in Kollontai's collection *Liubov' pchel trudovykh* (Moscow–Petrograd, 1923). It is translated by Cathy Porter in Alexandra Kollontai, *Love of Worker Bees* (London, 1977), pp. 182–211.

31. The evolution of the relationship can be closely traced in their correspondence. See Vladimir Mayakovsky, *Love is the Heart of Everything. Correspondence between Vladimir Mayakovsky and Lili Brik 1915–1930*, ed. Bengt Jangfeldt, trans. Julian Graffy (Edinburgh, 1986).

32. L. Brik, 'Iz vospominanii', *Druzhba narodov*, 3, 1989, pp. 186–217 (p. 209).

33. On the history of the streets see T. G. Pavlova, *Severnyi krai Moskvy (s drevneishikh vremen do 1917 goda)* (Moscow, 1998), pp. 40–1, 120–3, 296–325; and P. V. Sytin, *Iz istorii moskovskikh ulits* [1958] (Moscow, 2000), pp. 360–4. On the name 'Third Grazhdanskaia Street', see Korotkii, '"Tret'ia Meshchanskaia" Abrama Rooma', p. 55.

34. For a definition of the term '*meshchane*' roughly contemporaneous with *Bed and Sofa*, see the entry in *Bol'shaia Sovetskaia Entsiklopediia*, Vol. 39 (1938), col. 308.

35. V. Maiakovskii, 'O driani', in his *Polnoe sobranie sochinenii v trinadtsati tomakh* (henceforth Maiakovskii, *PSS*), Vol. 2, pp. 73–5.

36. A. M. Selishchev, *Iazyk revoliutsionnoi epokhi. Iz nabliudenii nad russkim iazykom poslednikh let (1917–1926)*, 2nd edn (Moscow, 1928), p. 193, where he alludes to Lenin's negative use of the term. Selishchev is quoted by

Sheila Fitzpatrick in her article 'The Problem of Class Identity in NEP Society', in S. Fitzpatrick, A. Rabinowitch and R. Stites (eds), *Russia in the Era of NEP. Explorations in Soviet Society and Culture* (Bloomington and Indianapolis, IN, 1991), pp. 12–33 (p. 18).

37. For an overview of the NEP period, see G. Hosking, 'The New Economic Policy and Its Political Dilemmas', in his *A History of the Soviet Union* (London, 1985), pp. 119–48; and R. Service, 'The New Economic Policy (1921–1928)', in his *A History of Twentieth-Century Russia* (London, 1997), pp. 123–49.

38. Fitzpatrick, 'The Problem of Class Identity in NEP Society', p. 21.

39. M. Liadov, *Voprosy byta* (Moscow, 1925), p. 8, cited in Naiman, *Sex in Public*, p. 158. For the NEP as a period of anxiety, see Naiman, *passim*.

40. V. Dunham, *In Stalin's Time. Middleclass Values in Soviet Fiction* [1976], rev. edn (Durham, NC and London, 1990), pp. 19–20. There is also a useful discussion of the debate about *meshchanstvo* in S. Boym, *Common Places. Mythologies of Everyday Life in Russia* (Cambridge, MA, and London, 1994), pp. 66–73.

41. This interpretation is referred to in two pieces by Nea Zorkaia, who ascribes it to the mathematician and civil rights activist, Leonid Pliushch. See 'K 100-letiiu Abrama Rooma. "Kruglyi stol" v Muzee kino', *Kinovedcheskie zapiski*, 24, 1994–95, pp. 163–74 (pp. 167–8); and N. Zorkaia, 'Gendernye problemy v sovetskom kino 30-kh [sic] godov. "Liubovnyi treugol'nik" kak kul'turologicheskaia i sotsiologicheskaia problema. (Kommentarii k "Tret'ei Meshchanskoi" A. Rooma)', in A. S. Troshin (ed.), *Close-Up. Istoriko-teoreticheskii seminar vo VGIKe* (Moscow, 1999), pp. 210–19 (p. 215). This reading, which Zorkaia herself considers forced, is associated with the prominence of the picture of Stalin behind the calendar on the wall of the flat, and leads Zorkaia ('Gendernye problemy', p. 215) to make the erroneous suggestion that the film is set in July 1927, and to refer to the major intra-Party struggle of that period. But the fact that the film was completed in 1926 and released on 15 March 1927 makes commentary on the events of July 1927 little short of miraculous. Zorkaia's vagueness over dates is also apparent in the very title of her article, which, with a similar interest in time-travel, considers the film as an example of gender problems in the 1930s!

42. The same image is used by Maiakovskii to suggest the dynamism of city life in his 1913 poem 'From Street to Street' [Iz ulitsy v ulitsu], in which 'A magician pulls the rails out of the jaws of a tram'; Maiakovskii, *PSS*, Vol. 1, p. 38.

43. Writing in 1930, Paul Rotha compared the rhythm of this sequence to the train at the opening of Walther Ruttmann's *Berlin – Symphony of a Great City* [Berlin: Die Sinfonie der Großstadt, 1927]. See P. Rotha, *The Film Till Now* [1930] (London, 1967), p. 392.

44. The scene is in *Doctor Zhivago*, Part 5, section 16, and is followed by another, set at the start of NEP, in Part 15, section 5. The cathedral was destroyed in December 1931, and rebuilt only in the 1990s.

45. We are never given a close-up of this picture. While most critics refer to it as coming from *Sovetskii ekran*, which first appeared on 24 March 1925, some call it *Ekran*, another film magazine which started to appear before the Revolution. While only the word *Ekran* is clearly visible, *Sovetskii ekran* used various formats for its logo, one of which, used for example in issue 7 for 1926, looks very similar to the one in the picture.

46. A. Room, 'Moi kinoubezhdeniia', first in *Sovetskii ekran*, 8, 1926, p. 5; quoted from Zabrodin (ed.), *Abram Matveevich Room. 1894–1976*, pp. 10–12 (p. 12).

47. V. Shklovskii, 'Pogranichnaia liniia' [*Kino*, 22 March 1927], in his *Za 60 let. Raboty o kino* (Moscow, 1985), pp. 110–13 (pp. 111–12).

48. Maiakovskii, *PSS*, Vol. 1, p. 156.

49. Quoted in A. Flaker, 'Byt', *Russian Literature,* 19, 1, 1986, pp. 1–13 (Tret'iakov, p. 2; Arvatov, pp. 2–3; Malevich, pp. 4–5).

50. Maiakovskii, *PSS*, Vol. 2, p. 75. Wrangel was a White general.

51. Ibid., Vol. 4, pp. 135–84 (pp. 160–5).

52. Quoted from Kollontai, *Love of Worker Bees*, pp. 69–70. See also B. Ingemanson, 'The Political Function of Domestic Objects in the Fiction of Aleksandra Kollontai', *Slavic Review*, 48, 1, 1989, pp. 71–82.

53. On this, and its link to the electrification campaign, see V. Buchli, 'Soviet Hygiene and the Battle Against Dirt and Petit-bourgeois Consciousness', chapter 3, pp. 41–62 of his *An Archaeology of Socialism* (Oxford and New York, 1999).

54. *Sovety proletarskoi khoziaike* (Ekaterinburg, 1924), pp. 90–1, quoted in Buchli, *An Archaeology of Socialism*, p. 44.

55. El' Lisitskii, 'Kul'tura zhil'ia' [1926], quoted in Boym, *Common Places*, p. 38. Lopukhov in *What is to be Done?* had also stripped his room of anything that was not absolutely necessary (see chapter 3, section 20 of the novel).

56. Boym, *Common Places*, pp. 35–8.

57. V. Tatlin, 'Problemy sootnosheniia cheloveka i veshchi: ob''iavim voinu komodam i bufetam', *Rabis*, 14 April 1930, p. 9, quoted in O. Matich, 'Remaking the Bed. Utopia in Daily Life', in J. Bowlt and O. Matich (eds), *Laboratory of Dreams. The Russian Avant-garde and Cultural Experiment* (Stanford, CA, 1996), pp. 59–78 (p. 60).

58. Buchli, *An Archaeology of Socialism*, pp. 44–5.

59. 'Dvinsk', in R. Taylor (ed.), *Beyond the Stars. The Memoirs of Sergei Eisenstein*, Vol. 4 of S. M. Eisenstein, *Selected Works* (London and Calcutta, 1995), pp. 138–9.

60. See the illustrations from *Lef*, 3, 1923, reproduced in Matich, 'Remaking the Bed', p. 71 and the design by Rodchenko, in ibid., p. 74.

61. Buchli, *An Archaeology of Socialism*, p. 44.

62. W. Benjamin, 'Moscow' [1927], in his *One-Way Street and Other Writings* (London, 1979), pp. 177–208 (p. 188). Boym, *Common Places*, pp. 130–4.

63. D. Crystal (ed.), *The Cambridge Factfinder*, 3rd edn (Cambridge, 1998), p. 148. See 'A Note on Dates', pp. x–xi.

64. For an evocation of life in the Red Cavalry during the Civil War, see Isaak Babel's story collection *Red Cavalry* [Konarmiia]. Kolia's association with the Red Cavalry is also indicated by his cavalry sword and binoculars on the wall.

65. Chernyshevsky, *What is to be Done?*, chapter 3, section 29.

66. See J. Bowlt, 'Body Beautiful: The Artistic Search for the Perfect Physique', in Bowlt and Matich (eds), *Laboratory of Dreams*, pp. 37–58.

67. This account of the new regime's attitude to physical exercise is taken from J. Riordan, *Sport in Soviet Society: Development of Sport and Physical Education in Russia and the USSR* (Cambridge, 1977), chapters 3 and 4; and from J. Read, 'Physical Culture and Sport in the Early Soviet Period', *Australian Slavonic and East European Studies*, 10, 1, 1996, pp. 59–84. See also T. Clark, 'The "New Man's" Body: A Motif in Early Soviet Culture', in M. Cullerne-Bown and B. Taylor (eds), *Art of the Soviets: Painting, Sculpture and Architecture in a One-party State 1917–1992* (Manchester and New York, 1993), pp. 33–50.

68. L. Attwood and C. Kelly, 'Programmes for Identity: the "New Man" and the "New Woman"', in C. Kelly and D. Shepherd (eds), *Constructing Russian Culture in the Age of Revolution: 1881–1940* (Oxford, 1998), pp. 256–90 (pp. 267–9).

69. On this, see F. Bernstein, 'Envisioning Health in Revolutionary Russia: the Politics of Gender in Sexual-Enlightenment Posters of the 1920s', *Russian Review*, 57, 2, 1998, pp. 191–217 (see especially the 1927 poster 'Physical Culture – the Weapon of the Class Struggle' illustrated on p. 200).

70. Maiakovskii, *PSS*, Vol. 7, p. 178.

71. Lenin quoted in K. Razlogov, '… Il' perechti "Zhenit´bu Figaro"', *Iskusstvo kino*, 6, 1999, pp. 25–9 (p. 27).

72. Compare frame enlargement 30 from early in the film, showing the building in all its grandeur, with its implosion in frame enlargement 213 in V. Petrić, *Constructivism in Film. The Man with the Movie Camera. A Cinematic Analysis* (Cambridge, 1987), pp. 255, 303.

73. On the difficulty of shooting this scene, which involved the cameraman sitting on the head of one of the horses, with the camera on the horse's back, see Giber, 'Kak snimalas´ "Tret´ia Meshchanskaia"'.

74. For Eric Naiman, 'Kolia reclines next to the petrified genitals of the statue of Apollo on the Bolshoi's roof. NEP, like the Medusa, turns man to lazy, contemptible, bourgeois stone' (Naiman, *Sex in Public*, p. 203, note 74).

75. Benjamin, *Moscow*, p. 189.

76. Maiakovskii, 'Prozasedavshiesia', *PSS*, Vol. 4, pp. 7–9.

77. Quoted in Naiman, *Sex in Public*, p. 92.

78. Quoted in ibid., p. 93.

79. Quoted in Buchli, *An Archaeology of Socialism*, p. 57.

80. There is a large and absorbing literature on the status of women in the decade after the Revolution. Of particular interest are W. Z. Goldman, *Women, the State and Revolution. Soviet Family Policy and Social Life, 1917–1936* (Cambridge, 1993); R. Stites, *The Women's Liberation Movement in Russia. Feminism, Nihilism and Bolshevism 1860–1930* [1978] (Princeton, NJ, 1991), especially the sections on 'Bolshevik Liberation', pp. 317–45, and 'The Sexual Revolution', pp. 346–91; B. Evans Clements, 'The Birth of the New Soviet Woman', in A. Gleason, P. Kenez and R. Stites, (eds), *Bolshevik Culture. Experiment and Order in the Russian Revolution* (Bloomington, IN, 1985), pp. 220–37; A. Chernykh, 'Sem'ia, byt i sotsial'nyi kontrol'', in her *Stanovlenie Rossii sovetskoi. 20–e gody v zerkale sotsiologii* (Moscow, 1998), pp. 169–214.

81. On the Zhenotdel, see especially Stites, *The Women's Liberation Movement in Russia*, pp. 329–45; B. Evans Clements, 'The Utopianism of the Zhenotdel', *Slavic Review*, 51, 3, 1992, pp. 485–96; and P. M. Chirkov's provocatively titled *Reshenie zhenskogo voprosa v SSSR (1917–1937 gg.)* (Moscow, 1978), pp. 53–61.

82. A. Kollontai, 'Revoliutsiia byta', first published in her *Trud zhenshchiny v evoliutsii khoziaistva* (Moscow–Petrograd, 1923); quoted in *Iskusstvo kino*, 6, 1991, pp. 105–9. On the evolution of Kollontai's views, see especially B. Evans Clements, *Bolshevik Feminist: The Life of Aleksandra Kollontai* (Bloomington, IN, 1979); and B. Brodsky Farnsworth, *Aleksandra Kollontai. Socialism, Feminism and the Bolshevik Revolution* (Stanford, CA, 1980).

83. Evans Clements, 'The Utopianism of the Zhenotdel', pp. 486–7.

84. Woman worker, letter to *Rabotnitsa*, 1918, quoted in ibid., p. 494.

85. X. Gasiorowska, *Women in Soviet Fiction, 1917–1964* (Madison, Milwaukee and London, 1968).

86. For a survey of the images of women in the cinema of the period see Ivan Dykhovichnyi's documentary film *A Woman's Role* [Zhenskaia rol', 1995].

87. Evans Clements, 'The Utopianism of the Zhenotdel', p. 490.

88. R. E. Johnson, 'Family Life in Moscow during NEP', in Fitzpatrick et al. (eds), *Russia in the Era of NEP*, pp. 106–24 (pp. 112, 116).

89. See A. Gorsuch, '"A Woman is not a Man": the Culture of Gender and Generation in Soviet Russia, 1921–1928', *Slavic Review*, 55, 3, 1996, pp. 636–60 (p. 646).

90. Gasiorowska, *Women in Soviet Fiction*, p. 95.

91. See the discussion between the couple in *What is to be Done?*, chapter 2, section 18. See also 'Everyone wants to have [...] a separate room for himself alone [...] the sanctity of a threshold no one has the right to cross', ibid., chapter 4, section 1.

92. Kollontai, *Love of Worker Bees*, p. 113

93. V. Woolf, *A Room of One's Own* [1928] (Harmondsworth, 1965), p. 93.

94. A. S. Pushkin, *Polnoe sobranie sochinenii v 10 tomakh*, 3rd edn (Moscow, 1962–65), Vol. 5, p. 47 (*Evgenii Onegin*, chapter 2, canto 25). When Tat'iana later moves to Moscow, she, too, is distressed by a view from the window consisting of 'a stable, a kitchen and a fence' (ibid., p. 159, chapter 7, canto 23).

95. D. W. Davis, 'Ozu's Mother', in D. Desser (ed.), *Ozu's Tokyo Story* (Cambridge, 1997), pp. 76–100 (p. 77).

96. K. Tsetkin [Zetkin], 'Iz zapisnoi knizhki' [1925], in *Vospominaniia o Vladimire Il'iche Lenine* (Moscow, 1957), Vol. 2, pp. 477–96 (p. 490).

97. L. Trotskii 'From the Old Family to the New' [1923] in Rosenberg (ed.), *Bolshevik Visions*, Part 1, pp. 77–83 (quotation on p. 79).

98. A. Kollontai, 'The Family and the Communist State', quoted in ibid., pp. 67–76.

99. In this context it is interesting that Shklovskii had a famous quarrel with Lili Brik at a meeting of LEF, during which he called her a 'housewife' [domokhoziaika]. See I. Svetlikova, '"Gubernator zakhvachennykh territorii". (Osip Brik v razgovorakh Viktora Shklovskogo s Aleksandrom Chudakovym)', *Novoe literaturnoe obozrenie*, 41, 2000, pp. 99–107 (p. 105).

100. Semenova, 'Zhizn' snachala ... ', p. 323.

101. The Russian lexicographer Vladimir Dal' lists the many Russian sayings about cats. In the context of the scene of the cat washing in the opening sequence and the later development of the plot, it is interesting to note that several of the sayings compiled by Dal' associate a cat washing with the arrival of a guest. See V. Dal', *Tolkovyi slovar' zhivogo velikorusskogo iazyka*, 4th edn, Vol. 2 (St Petersburg and Moscow, 1914), columns 467–8. If the cat thus stands for Volodia, then it is a hint of Kolia's later complacency and responsibility for his own betrayal that he literally flings it in Liuda's face. The cat's connection with Volodia is continued later in the film, where it is often seen lying on his sofa, and in this context it is important that the cat can also signify sensuality.

102. Tsetkin [Zetkin], 'Iz zapisnoi knizhki', pp. 489–90.

103. Woolf, *A Room of One's Own*, p. 87.

104. See Iutkevich, 'Kak ia stal rezhisserom', p. 322. The town of Briansk lies to the south-west of Moscow, not far from the Belorussian and Ukrainian borders.

105. For details on where Volodia walks, see M. Turovskaia, '"Zhenskii fil'm" – chto eto takoe?', *Iskusstvo kino*, 5, 1981, pp. 28–35; reprinted in her *Pamiati tekushchego mgnoveniia* (Moscow, 1987), pp. 246–62 (p. 252); and Grashchenkova, *Abram Room*, p. 100. The Freedom Obelisk was designed by the architect Dmitri Osipov and the sculptor Nikolai Andreev, and was installed on the first anniversary of the Revolution where the statue of General Skobelev had previously stood. Volodia's association with it is one of several indications of his modernity. The

monument was demolished in April 1941. See Timothy J. Colton, *Moscow. Governing the Socialist Metropolis* (Cambridge, MA and London, 1995), pp. 108–10. There is a photograph of the Moscow City Soviet building and the obelisk, contemporary with the film, on page 109. Neither Kolia nor Liuda will actually be shown walking through Moscow.

106. See the jacket illustration and figure 4. 2, in J. Mayne, *Kino and the Woman Question. Feminism and Soviet Silent Film* (Columbus, OH, 1989), p. 117.

107. Fitzpatrick, 'The Problem of Class Identity in NEP Society', p. 16.

108. See the section 'Fantasies of the War Communist Body', in Naiman, *Sex in Public*, pp. 57–78.

109. On this see E. Waters, 'The Female Form in Soviet Political Iconography, 1917–1932', in B. Evans Clements, B. Alpern Engel and C. D. Worobec (eds), *Russia's Women: Accommodation, Resistance, Transformation* (Berkeley, CA, 1991), pp. 225–42; and V. Bonnell, 'The Representation of Women in Early Soviet Political Art', *Russian Review*, 50, 3, 1991, pp. 267–88.

110. Iutkevich recalls filming the entire printing process, including Fogel's hair, at the printers of *Sovetskii ekran*, which he knew well, though not everything they shot went into the final film (Iutkevich, 'Kak ia stal rezhisserom', p. 324).

111. Lenin quoted in Chernykh, *Stanovlenie Rossii sovetskoi*, p. 196.

112. M. Bulgakov, *Sobranie sochinenii v piati tomakh* (Moscow, 1989–90), Vol. 2, p. 137. *The Heart of a Dog* was banned in the Soviet Union until 1987.

113. See the entries on 'zhilishchno-sanitarnaia norma' and 'zhilishche' in *Bol'shaia Sovetskaia Entsiklopediia*, Vol. 25 (1932), columns 451, 453, 502.

114. P. Kozhanyi, *Zhilishchnyi vopros i zhilishchnaia kooperatsiia* (Moscow, 1925), p. 11. For a recent assessment of housing conditions in the 1920s, see Chernykh, *Stanovlenie Rossii sovetskoi*, pp. 195–210.

115. Bulgakov, *Sobranie sochinenii v piati tomakh*, Vol. 5, p. 123.

116. Benjamin, 'Moscow', pp. 187–8; *Moscow Diary*, p. 104.

117. See Chernyshevskii, *What is to be Done?*, chapter 2, section 7, and later, chapter 3, section 4, for Vera Pavlovna giving educational readings to her workers at the sewing workshop.

118. See the entry on 'radioveshchanie' in *Bol'shaia Sovetskaia Entsiklopediia*, Vol. 47 (1941), columns 55–9.

119. Benjamin, *Moscow Diary*, p. 112, and see the illustration on p. 113.

120. Grashchenkova, *Abram Room*, p. 8.

121. See, for example, 'Cine-Pravda and Radio-Pravda' ['"Kinopravda" i "Radiopravda"', 1925], in Taylor and Christie (eds), *The Film Factory*, pp. 129–31. Radios and radio broadcasts figure in Vertov's films *The*

Kino-Eye. Life Caught Unawares, The Man with the Movie-Camera, Enthusiasm/Symphony of the Donbass and *Three Songs of Lenin*.

122. On the history of these societies, see W. E. Odom, *The Soviet Volunteers: Modernization and Bureaucracy in a Public Mass Organization* (Princeton, NJ, 1973), from which these details are taken.

123. It is not clear whether this is the result of an accident, or some kind of exercise. According to Zorkaia, 'Gendernye problemy', p. 214, this sequence originally included an 'aerial parade' and an appearance by Marshal Budennyi.

124. Writing about the effect of aerial photography in 1925, Shklovskii had argued that in such shots herds of animals look like shards of a broken pot and houses like bread rolls. People seen from the air were deprived of personal fates. See Shklovskii, '"Velikii perelet" i kinematografiia' [*Kino*, 8 December 1925], in his *Za 60 let*, pp. 76–7 (p. 77).

125. This account and all the examples are taken from F. Wigzell, *Reading Russian Fortunes. Print Culture, Gender and Divination in Russia from 1765* (Cambridge, 1998), pp. 117–23.

126. In the epigraph to Pushkin's eponymous story, the Queen of Spades is said to denote 'secret malevolence', and this meaning has since been widely associated with the card. See Pushkin, *Polnoe sobranie sochinenii v 10 tomakh*, Vol. 6, p. 317.

127. This information is taken from G. G. Pospelov, *Bubnovyi valet. Primitiv i gorodskoi fol'klor v moskovskoi zhivopisi 1910-kh godov* (Moscow, 1990), p. 99. The quotations from *The Idiot* are from F. Dostoevskii, *Polnoe sobranie sochinenii v tridtsati tomakh*, Leningrad, 1972–1990, Volume 8, p. 104.

128. It has recently been suggested that Vladimir Nabokov may have seen *Bed and Sofa* in Berlin, where the film had an enormous success (see below, chapter 3), while working on his triangle novel *King, Queen, Knave* [Korol', dama, valet], which he completed in Berlin in June 1928. In the novel the characters are associated with specific playing cards and cards are also associated with fortune-telling. See Andrei Rogachevski, '"Korol', (pikovaia) dama, valet": k voprosu o pushkinskom fone u Nabokova', in I. Belobrovtseva and A. Danilevskii (eds), *Kul'tura russkoi diaspory: Vladimir Nabokov – 100. Materialy nauchnoi konferentsii (Tallinn-Tartu, 14–17 ianvaria 1999)* (Tallinn, 2000), pp. 276–97 (pp. 282–3).

129. The poster shows, from left to right, the Jack of Hearts, Queen of Clubs and King of Diamonds (see Plate 10). In the Stenberg brothers' poster, the cards are in the corner: the King of Hearts, the Queen of Clubs and the Jack of Hearts (see Plate 5). Thus in neither poster are the cards exactly as in the film. Both posters, playing on the film's title, announce that Fogel plays the part of 'Tretii', 'The Third'. Cartomancy as a way of deciding whom to marry also features in Pabst's *Diary of a Lost Girl*, 1929.

130. There are extracts from the Family Code of 1918 in R. Schlesinger (ed.), *The Family in the USSR. Documents and Readings* (London, 1949), pp. 33–41. There is a very useful discussion of the provisions of this code in Goldman, *Women, the State and Revolution*, pp. 48–58.

131. For these and other provisions see the extracts from the Family Code of 1926 in Schlesinger (ed.), *The Family in the USSR*, pp. 154–68, which is preceded by lengthy extracts from the discussion of the draft code, pp. 81–153. Among the most useful discussions of the 1926 code and preparations for it are those in Goldman, *Women, the State and Revolution*, pp. 185–253; B. Brodsky Farnsworth, 'Bolshevik Alternatives and the Soviet Family: the 1926 Marriage Law Debate', in D. Atkinson, A. Dallin and G. Warshofsky Lapidus (eds), *Women in Russia* (Stanford, CA, 1977; Hassocks, 1978), pp. 139–65; and T. Osipovich, 'Problemy pola, braka, sem'i i polozhenie zhenshchiny v obshchestvennykh diskussiiakh serediny 20-kh godov', *Obshchestvennye nauki i sovremennost'*, 1, 1994, pp. 161–71.

132. In fact it says, erroneously, 'Saturday the 9th'. For an explanation on this inconsistency, see 'A Note on Dates', pp. x–xi.

133. N. Krupskaia, *Vospominaniia o Lenine* (Moscow, 1933), p. 280, quoted in Chirkov, *Reshenie zhenskogo voprosa v SSSR*, p. 218.

134. See figure 4. 1, in Mayne, *Kino and the Woman Question*, p. 117. There is an interesting discussion of this patterning, ibid., pp. 115–16. Similar patterning is used to startling effect in Aleksandr Rodchenko's famous 1934 photograph 'The girl with the Leica'; see A. M. Rodchenko, *Stat'i. Vospominaniia. Avtobiograficheskie zapiski. Pis'ma* (Moscow, 1982), illustration 92.

135. In François Truffaut's film about a triangular love affair, *Jules et Jim* (discussed below), Jules and Jim are repeatedly seen engaged in a game of dominoes, from which Catherine tries in vain to distract them.

136. 'Toska! Tak den' za dnem idet v uedinen'e! / No esli pod vecher v pechal'noe selen'e, / Kogda za shashkami sizhu ia v ugolke ... ', Pushkin, *Polnoe sobranie sochinenii v 10 tomakh*, Vol. 3, p. 128.

137. See frame enlargements 185 and 186 in Petrić, *Constructivism in Film*, p. 295.

138. See Riordan, *Sport in Soviet Society*, p. 61.

139. Benjamin, *Moscow Diary*, p. 63.

140. The references are to be found in Maiakovskii, *PSS*, Vol. 1, p. 159, and Vol. 4, p. 158.

141. Aleksandr Blok, *Sobranie sochinenii v 8 tomakh* (Moscow–Leningrad, 1960–1965), volume 2, pp. 185–6.

142. C. Pateman, 'The Fraternal Social Contract', quoted in Gorsuch, 'A Woman is not a Man', p. 650. Gorsuch's article looks at the way masculine comradeship worked towards the marginalisation of women in the Komsomol.

143. Mayne, *Kino and the Woman Question*, pp. 119–21.

144. E. Kosofsky Sedgwick, *Between Men: English Literature and Male Homosocial Desire* (New York, 1985); quoted in J. Rivkin and M. Ryan (eds), *Literary Theory. An Anthology* (Oxford, 1998), pp. 696–712 (p. 708). Kosofsky Sedgwick is offering a reading of Girard's study *Deceit, Desire and the Novel*.

145. Kosofsky Sedgwick, quoted in Rivkin and Ryan (eds), *Literary Theory*, pp. 710–11.

146. Zorkaia, 'Gendernye problemy', pp. 216–19. Zorkaia of course makes much of the kiss between the men earlier in the film, but the kiss is clearly presented as a joke, and to read it despite that as evidence of (perhaps unacknowledged) homosexual desire seems to provide a disablingly oversimplified analysis.

147. A. Smith and C. England, *An Evening with Gary Lineker* (London, 1993), p. 51.

148. On the NEP and the Gothic motif of the heroine behind the locked door, see Naiman, *Sex in Public*, pp. 152–3.

149. When Volodia gets up Giber offers a close-up of an empty carafe of water on the table. Some critics have suggested that this is an allusion to the so-called 'glass of water' theory of sexual relationships, according to which sexual desire was a simple physiological need that could be simply 'slaked', which was widely discussed (and variously attributed) at the time. But this would seem to run counter to the subtlety with which the feelings between the couple are shown at this point in the film. On the source of the metaphor, see, for example, Naiman, *Sex in Public*, p. 248.

150. Iurii Olesha, *Izbrannoe* (Moscow, 1974), pp. 93–4. On the theme of the 'sharing' of a single woman by a group of men in Soviet fiction of the period, see Naiman, *Sex in Public*, p. 280.

151. Kollontai, 'The Family and the Communist State', quoted in Rosenberg (ed.), *Bolshevik Visions*, Part 1, p. 75.

152. See, in M. Ilic, *Women Workers in the Soviet Interwar Economy. From 'Protection' to 'Equality'* (London, 1998), chapter 5, 'Maternity', pp. 57–77, and Appendix 1, 'Summary of Decrees', pp. 177–82.

153. N. V. Shchepkin, *Okhrana materi i rebenka po nashim zakonam. Kratkii spravochnik dlia materei* (Moscow, 1927). The quotations are taken from p. 10.

154. Gorsuch, '"A Woman is not a Man"', p. 650.

155. In this sense the baby is reduced to the status of the corset which the hero cannot get rid of in Eduard Puchal'skii's pre-Revolutionary comedy *Antosha Ruined by a Corset* [Antoshu korset pogubil, 1916], a film which was banned by the Repertory Committee in 1926 as, 'A stupid and empty comedy with vulgar episodes scattered through it'. See '"Kartina makhrovo-meshchanskaia. Peredelke ne poddaetsia ... " Iz protokolov

repertuarnoi komissii 1926–1927 gg. (Chast' vtoraia)', publ. and notes N. A. Dymshits, *Kinovedcheskie zapiski*, 45, 2000, pp. 57–101 (pp. 58–9).

156. On *Kat'ka, Bumazhnyi ranet* see N. Nusinova, 'Novaia Eva', *Iskusstvo kino*, 6, 1993, pp. 129–34 (p. 132); and Attwood and Kelly, 'Programmes for Identity: the "New Man" and the "New Woman"', pp. 276–8.

157. For the tale of real-life Komsomol behaviour that was one of Ermler's sources for the film see Naiman, *Sex in Public*, pp. 280–1.

158. Liudmila Semenova plays the part of a neighbour in this film.

159. This information on abortion in the Soviet Union is taken from the excellent accounts provided in W. Z. Goldman, 'Women, Abortion and the State, 1917–1936', in Evans Clements et al. (eds), *Russia's Women: Accommodation, Resistance, Transformation*, pp. 243–66; Goldman, *Women, the State and Revolution*, pp. 254–95; and N. Lebina, 'Abortmakher v podpol'e', *Rodina*, 1, 1991, pp. 47–51. The text of the law banning abortion in 1936 and extracts from the discussions that took place that year are in Schlesinger (ed.), *The Family in the USSR. Documents and Readings*, pp. 251–79.

160. Shchepkin, *Okhrana materi i rebenka po nashim zakonam*, pp. 12–13.

161. There is an interesting discussion of the implications of the two women's different views from the window in Mayne, *Kino and the Woman Question*, pp. 122–3.

162. This information is taken from Bernstein, 'Envisioning Health in Revolutionary Russia'. See especially the illustrations on pp. 197 and 213.

163. See Grashchenkova, *Abram Room*, p. 107.

164. See, for example, P. E. Burns, 'An NEP Moscow Address: Abram Room's *Third Meshchanskaia (Bed and Sofa)* in Historical Context', *Film and History*, 12, 4, 1982, pp. 73–81 (p. 78).

165. M. Haskell, *From Reverence to Rape* [1974] (Chicago, IL, 1987), see pp. 320–1.

166. N. Iakovlev, 'Pervosortnaia meshchanskaia', *Kino*, 5, 29 January 1927, p. 3; Burns, 'An NEP Moscow Address', pp. 77–8.

167. Goldman, *Women, the State and Revolution*, especially chapter 6, 'Sexual Freedom or Social Chaos: the Debate on the 1926 Code', pp. 214–53.

168. Kollontai, *Love of Worker Bees*, p. 175.

169. The play had its world première in Karlsruhe in 1976, but the text of *I Want a Child!* was not published in the Soviet Union until 1988: S. Tret'iakov, 'Khochu rebenka', *Sovremennaia dramaturgiia*, 2, 1988, pp. 206–37.

170. Meierkhol'd's words are quoted in ibid., p. 208.

171. The materials of the discussion of the play are printed in *Sovremennaia dramaturgiia*, 2, 1988, pp. 238–43. Room's words are on p. 239. There is a discussion of the fate of the play in Naiman, *Sex in Public*, pp. 109–14.

172. Grashchenkova, *Abram Room*, p. 126.

173. Shchepkin, *Okhrana materi i rebenka po nashim zakonam*, pp. 19–20.

174. Grashchenkova, *Abram Room*, p. 107.

175. Chernyshevsky, *What is to be Done?*, chapter 4, section 11.

176. A. Kollontai, 'Brak, zhenshchiny i alimenty', *Ekran*, 5, 1926, p. 1. Information on this article is taken from Farnsworth, 'Bolshevik Alternatives and the Soviet Family', pp. 151, 155–6.

177. This scene offers a neat upending of the scene of the two Young Communist League members turning up at the maternity hospital in the real-life source used by Shklovskii. See above, pp. 14–15.

178. See, for example, Korotkii, '"Tret′ia Meshchanskaia" Abrama Rooma', pp. 36–7.

179. V. Shklovskii, in his *Podenshchina* (Leningrad, 1930), p. 87; quoted in Nusinova, 'Novaia Eva', pp. 130–1.

180. Naiman, *Sex in Public*, p. 239. See also ibid., p. 181.

181. Ibid., p. 47.

182. On this see, for example, R. Taylor, 'But "Eastward, look, the land is brighter": Towards a Topography of Utopia in the Stalinist Musical', in D. Holmes and A. Smith (eds), *Entertaining Ideologies: Reflections on 100 Years of European Cinema* (Manchester, 2000), pp. 11–25.

183. See Evans Clements, 'The Utopianism of the Zhenotdel', pp. 492–3.

184. The oath is quoted from Buchli, *An Archaeology of Socialism*, p. 61.

3. After *Bed and Sofa*: The Reception of the Film and the Fate of Its Themes

The Film's Initial Reception in the Soviet Union

Bed and Sofa was completed by the end of 1926. Though the film was not released officially until 15 March 1927, previews must already have been taking place, for by January press discussion was intense.[1] Writing in the first issue for 1927 of *Kinofront*, the journal of the Association of Revolutionary Cinematography [ARK], with which Room had close connections, K. Ganzenko found it to be 'the first film of contemporary Soviet life that is successfully executed from beginning to end'; and felt that Batalov 'gives a fine portrayal of the self-enamoured husband, the simple fellow who has become petit-bourgeois [omeshchanivshegosia], who has retreated into himself, but who will accommodate to any circumstance'.[2]

Viktor Pertsov reported on audience reaction:

> If *Third Meshchanskaia Street* is an undoubted success for Soviet cinema, the director still gets asked: 'Do the majority of the working class in the USSR really live in a flat like that?', or 'Have you ever seen the working class drink tea out of a glass holder [podstakannika]?', or 'Is it really possible that a proletarian husband, learning that his wife had been unfaithful, would just leave his wife and his living space without resorting to a fight?'

But he goes on to suggest that the director of a film about daily life should know how to expose its dialectics, rather than reducing it to a diagram. If he does not do this he will have nothing to hold on to professionally.[3]

On 17 January 1927 ARK held a meeting to discuss the film, and the resolution they drew up after the discussion praised the filmmakers for their readiness to place the story in the thick of contemporary life; for the realism of their approach; for the subtlety of the direction of individual scenes; for the 'tactful resolution of key episodes in the picture, absolutely without any tendency towards pornography'; and for the bold and artistic elaboration of the details of everyday life and the influence of *meshchanstvo*. They did consider that the set design was perhaps too elaborate, and that this disadvantaged the actors. They felt that Liuda's change in character could have been articulated in more detail. They concluded:

> The director A. Room has coped fully with the complex task of filming Soviet daily life.
>
> The film *Third Meshchanskaia Street* successfully overturns the prevailing opinion that Soviet life is 'uncinematographic'. The picture opens the way to the wide use of plots taken from Soviet life as material for feature films.
>
> The film *Third Meshchanskaia Street*, while posing one of the most acute questions of Soviet life – the relationship between the sexes and marital and family life – is absolutely correct to refuse to resolve them finally, posing the question in a soft, artistic and restrainedly Soviet form to be discussed by the viewers themselves.
>
> The artistic virtues of the picture make it possible to pronounce it one of the most successful Soviet productions.

This resolution was affirmed by the members and colleagues of ARK on 8 February 1927 and published in a later issue of *Kinofront*.[4]

Pavel Bliakhin, a scriptwriter and Sovkino official, writing on 22 January, took issue with those who berated the film for merely posing questions and not answering them. 'Who, in our transitional era, when the old and new *byt* are intertwined, can give ready recipes for every day of life (except fools, of course)? We can see in only the most general outline the paths which the new *byt*, the new family and new relationships are taking.' Despite some doubts about the heroine, he also praised the triumph of the maternal instinct.[5]

A week later, on Saturday 29 January, *Sovetskii ekran* and *Kino* each carried two pieces about the film. In *Sovetskii ekran* Grigori Giber reported on the filming process in a piece that was illustrated with a montage of Moscow exteriors and a shot of the crew on the roof of the Bolshoi Theatre.[6] But on the previous page of the magazine was a highly disapproving review, full of demonstrable inaccuracies and blinded by its own censoriousness to what the film was really saying, by Konstantin Denisov: 'In a lyrical tone, in sunny bright colours under the fig leaf of a 100% decent Soviet ending, we are offered a practical, graphic recipe for a ... "ménage à trois" [...] Almost Room's basic task in this film was the defence of an undeveloped woman, a housewife.' Sardonically suggesting that Room has already proved himself a connoisseur of women through the prostitutes he depicted in *The Traitor*, he goes on to conclude that the character of Liuda is not so different:

> Every housewife in any working family has a whole poem [sic] of pots, primus stoves, wash-tubs, accounts, fears and so on. Her joys and sadnesses are those of her husband, the builder of life. The first thing we notice about Room's housewife is her exaggeratedly seductive rounded hips, the calm caresses of her figure, the calm imperiousness of her movements and ... that's all. She has but one concern: to gratify the tiniest whim of her husband the male; her sadnesses are lack of attention to her, the female. And this typical kept female, who knows no other cares than masculine whim, who in the hunt for a more attractive male moves from one man to another, is suddenly, don't you see, unhappy that this other man too turns out to be a male in his treatment of her, the female.[7]

Kino, too, had two articles about the film, one negative, the other positive, and both explicitly advertised as discussion pieces. In the view of Nikolai Iakovlev, who was the editor of *Sovetskii ekran*, Room had reduced 'the struggle between the old and new *byt* to a psychopathological ménage à trois' with elements of pornography. He further insisted: 'Room does not resolve either *in a Soviet way or in a revolutionary way* even a small part of this theme about a "ménage à trois".' Yet, Iakovlev continued, Soviet cinema should be 'actively building the new way of life – socialism' rather than 'coddling misfits like those depicted in *Third Meshchanskaia Street*'. For 'there could have been a way out – a clichéd one – which is alimony and the expulsion of the husbands from the "living space".[8]

In the other article in this issue of *Kino*, Khrisanf Khersonsky described *Bed and Sofa* as unusual, bold and original, since it broke with the tradition of cooking up films that are equally comprehensible to everyone according to a primitive propaganda recipe. According to Khersonsky the film's theme cannot be easily and simply resolved. *Meshchanstvo* is everywhere in contemporary Soviet *byt*; it is a moth which lurks in the homes of officials and bureaucrats, of workers and the intelligentsia, even of revolutionary fighters. Battling with it is complex; it needs to be subjected to a profound cultural offensive. Khersonsky contends that 'Shklovsky and Room have tried to cast light on a little corner of *meshchanstvo* if not yet with Lenin's search light, then at least with Chekhov's lamp'. He rejects with indignation the view that the film treats of an atypical case and the suggestion, made by some speakers at the ARK discussion, that Room's only target was workers who have succumbed to *petit-bourgeois* comfort. Listing the many vices of contemporary life that the film addresses, Khersonsky compares Room's approach to the ironic tone of a story by Chekhov. He asserts that Room offers no prescription, but the film *does* contain propaganda. It shows the viewer how the two men, 'who in general are fine fellows and our good and close friends', also turn out to be scoundrels. Liuda is right to leave, and it is up to the viewer to decide why, where to and what should be done about it. ('Chto nado delat´?', the eternal Russian question.) For Khersonsky it is the great virtue of the film that it is open-ended, and leaves the viewer to think about the conditions of contemporary Soviet life. The discussion in ARK showed both how contemporary and relevant the film is, and also that 'you have to learn how to look at a film – which is not an utterly simple matter'.[9]

On 5 February *Sovetskii ekran* carried a picture of Liuda's face with the criss-cross patterning of light and shade on its cover,[10] and responses to the film continued to appear throughout the month. Osip Beskin (later to be a leading Socialist Realist art critic) attacked the production company, Sovkino, which he accused of being responsible for reintroducing the provocative title *Ménage à trois* [Liubov´ vtroem] for Soviet distribution, and described the film as a Soviet *Woman of Paris* and a 'Western European adulterous romance'.[11]

In March, with the release of the film now imminent, interest grew even greater. On 5 March *Sovetskii ekran* printed a doggerel poem by 'Argo', which, punning on the fact that the word '*pol*' means both sex and floor in Russian, said that Room had become sex-crazed [svikhnuvshiisia na polovom voprose]; he used to have a good head on his shoulders, but now he combs his hair with a broom [shchetkoi polovoi].[12] Three days later, an article appeared in Leningrad, under the title 'Scoundrels, it seems'. It praised the film for showing what neither literature nor painting had yet been able to show, and for its extreme truth to life: 'The film contains no lofty gestures or lofty words about the equal rights of women, but every [household] pot in it speaks more than any slogan. In its entire essence this work summons the Liudmilas in the cinema auditorium to abandon their own Third Meshchanskaia Streets.'[13] At the same time, the pseudonymous 'Sha' attacked the film's open ending, and attacked ARK for approving it. Sha insisted that:

Art is organically incapable of being impartial; the artistic depiction of any fact is already a relationship to it. And if a fact in this depiction is not coloured by a specific, conscious tendency, then the 'objectivity' of the depiction sounds in the viewer's mind like a positive colouring of what is a specifically negative fact.

The acceptance by the Association of *Revolutionary* Cinematography of *such* a method of showing Soviet life as positive is typical of ARK in the sense that this social organisation has departed from its basic tasks and principles.[14]

Sergei Eisenstein, the directors Georgi and Sergei Vasilev, and Konstantin Iukov, the chairman of ARK, were among the signatories of a later letter in defence of the ARK line on the film, which reiterated that it opened new possibilities for Soviet cinema.[15]

Bed and Sofa was released on Tuesday, 15 March 1927. In the next six months it was seen by 1,260,560 viewers.[16] A large number of new reviews naturally appeared in the following days and weeks, and they continued to display a wide range of critical opinion. The worker-correspondent Mikhail Bystritsky attacked the film as un-Soviet, and argued that it contained no real characters capable of evoking an emotional response in the viewer. He felt that Soviet reality offered very rich material in the area of sexual relations, which 'the liberating tendency of the October Revolution' had forced to take on new forms, but, like several of his predecessors, insisted: 'In order to show questions of everyday life convincingly and to resolve them correctly' (something that Room had explicitly refused to do, and that more perceptive reviewers considered impossible) 'seeing is not enough, you must also be in a position to display a definite attitude to what you show.'[17] Valerin, on the other hand, praised the film for the delicacy with which it showed the emptiness of Liuda's life and the precision of its psychological analysis of the behaviour of the men. Valerin is certain that viewers will think Liuda right to leave the 'sadness of the life of a bourgeois family'. He continues:

> The value of the film lies in its posing on screen the problem of family life just as it is posed in daily reality, and in the fact that it propagandises the destruction of the bourgeois family [...] The director has exposed very well the complex links of the life of the past, with all the weight of ancient habits and traditions, and the new Soviet life.[18]

The *Pravda* reviewer, A. Zuev, attacked the 'enticing' title, *Ménage à trois* [Liubov' vtroem], which he said had been thought up for the poster. He conceded that the idea of 'posing' the problem of sexual relations was seductive, but it was also a difficult task, and Room and Shklovsky had not coped adequately with it. They had taken the line of least resistance and apathetically failed to take a position, failed above all to address the role of society. Room should have shown that the resolution of the problem of *meshchanstvo* lies, 'as everyone now knows', in the economic liberation of women, but he failed to do so, and thus the film remained a run-of-the-mill family drama, dominated by chance. Zuev praised the acting, though he felt that Semenova is forced to sit a little too long at the window. He nevertheless considered it a mistake to have the men come over as 'wonderful fellows [...] who are suffering innocently in the narrow circle of *byt*', and the wife as a noble heroine. The film failed both as 'Ménage à trois' and as 'Third Meshchanskaia Street' primarily because it lacks a social pivot; but it was exceptionally well made, with taste, wit and a fine attention to the Moscow exteriors. From this external point of view the work of both director and cameraman was beyond reproach.[19]

The same day, *Kino* carried a report of a discussion at which Room had been present after a showing of the film at the Society of Friends of Soviet Cinema [Obshchestvo druzei sovetskogo kino]. The society, the first mass cinema organisation for the Soviet public, had been founded, on ARK's initiative, in November 1925.[20] Room reminded his audience that nine-tenths of current film production was on historical themes, since contemporary subjects offered no colourful heroics, just ordinary people. He presented his film as a first attempt to address 'our grey day-to-day life' and hoped that his experience would lead to the making of better films. His humility did nothing to placate his audience. Anoshchenko, from the Moscow Association of Proletarian Writers, wanted the social dimension to be highlighted as an explanation of the family breakdown. Potemkin, a worker-correspondent of the newspaper *Rabochaia gazeta* (the paper Kolia reads in the film and the place where Volodia works), complained first that he could not work out whose *byt* this was – were they workers or intelligentsia or somewhere between? – and then that the sexual question is left unresolved. Kochetkov, another worker-correspondent on the same paper, could not understand how Volodia could come into someone else's flat and take over, and asked, rhetorically, was Liudmila a *meshchanka* or a prostitute? Faibusova, from the Political Enlightenment Section, called the picture 'false', insisting that 'we' do not live like this.[21]

The following day, the critic and scriptwriter Mikhail Bleiman called the film 'evidence of the gigantic growth of Soviet film art',[22] but, alas, this was not the view of the Red Army soldiers (we recall that both the film's heroes are ex-Red Army men) from the Political Section of the Special Troops of the Moscow and Moscow Region Garrison, expressed during a discussion after a showing of the film. All but one of the speakers were negative. They praised the fact that this important theme had been addressed, that the characters were real people and not theoretical constructs, that the film was very well made; but they did not find it true to life, and felt that it reduced the problem to an anecdote. Once again they were confused as to whether the heroes were workers or *petit-bourgeois* [meshchane]. They found that the film was contradictory and muddled [sumburnaia],[23] contained 'nothing organically Soviet', and was marked by 'a coating of vulgarity moving into pornography' (they cited the scene with the cards), which negated its achievements. Since 'The film gives nothing educational', the Red Army could do without it. One discussant felt that it could be shown to soldiers, but would need an introductory speech; others felt that this would not help and that the film was 'empty'. Room, present at the discussion, asked for some indulgence, repeating that his intention was not to resolve the question, but to force people to think about it.[24]

Reporting in the labour newspaper *Trud* the next day on the wide discussion of the film among workers, Red Army soldiers, cinema specialists and ordinary film fans, and noting that all the cinematically unsophisticated spectators had stressed the absence of the social dimension in the film, N.V. insisted that they were right to do so. He himself described it as an 'algebraic equation' according to a French model, with no attention to Soviet psychology. Though the acting, the direction, and the scenes of Moscow were excellent, the film lacked psychological profundity, included 'pornographic' details, contained nothing enriching, and the life it showed was a 'myth'.[25]

Nor did *Bed and Sofa* satisfy Shklovsky's LEF colleague Nikolai Chuzhak, who felt that it followed the French model of the *comédie larmoyante*, or tearful comedy, linking 'fatal questions' and *meshchanstvo*. For Chuzhak the film itself was marked by philistinism, neither positive nor negative in its approach, internally unresolved, false in its setting and in its psychology, and did not even pose its question properly. He was exercised by the ambiguity (which Shklovsky and Room clearly intended) of the class setting: on the one hand this seemed to be a working family, in which the wife even did her own laundry, and yet, on the other hand, there were elements of NEP influence in the room, the clothes, the food. He was unhappy about the character development: 'both men are wonderful fellows; you really don't know which of them is the nicer'; and yet they would turn out to be scoundrels. As for the woman – a flirt who reads her fortune at cards 'by some miracle at the end turns into a feminist!' (*feministku*; this is the only use of this term I have encountered in the contemporary Soviet reviews), which is an obvious device. Chuzhak ends his review, like so many other ideologically driven critics, by bemoaning the film's open ending, through which Room 'alas [...] cut off the final ideological branch on which he seemed to be sitting relatively firmly', leaving Liuda, in the reviewer's fervid imagination, probably about to embark upon a new *ménage à trois* on *Fourth* Meshchanskaia Street.[26]

In the last days of March, L. Vulfov declared in *Kino*: 'the bed and the sofa that stand in the room – these are the real heroes of the picture.'[27] Denise J. Youngblood has calculated, on the basis of the disappearance of advertisements from the press, that the film may have been withdrawn from first-run Moscow cinemas by this time, though, as she admits, this suggestion runs counter to attendance figures over six months of almost 1.3 million. Certainly, as has already been seen, the film provoked very contrary opinions. In one assessment it was given a viewer approval rating of only 25 per cent and made the 'most hated' list; on the other hand it was approved by Agitprop as suitable for workers and was apparently popular with bourgeois viewers (who were seemingly inattentive to the subtleties of its rendering of their lives).[28] It is also clear that active discussion of the film continued throughout April and into May 1927.

One opinion published in April is of particular interest. Osip Brik, whose triangular relationship with his wife Lili and the poet Maya-kovsky was widely thought to have been one of the sources of Shklovsky's screenplay, wrote about the film in *Kino*. Like Room, Brik felt that a key task of Soviet cinema was to make films about modern Soviet life and regretted the fact that a lack of confidence in the treatment of modern material meant that 80 per cent of contemporary productions were about 'Ivan the Terrible, Alexander I and other non-Soviet citizens'. He praised *Bed and Sofa* for finally tackling important contemporary issues, but called it 'half a victory' since the characters are inactive and lacking in strength of will (and not censured for this by the film-makers), and, most importantly, since their private life is shown outside its social context. He nevertheless concluded that even a partially successful film on a contemporary social theme would do infinitely more for Soviet cinema than yet another historical drama.[29]

In a survey tellingly entitled 'the petit-bourgeoisification [omesh-chanivanie] of Soviet film', published in *Izvestiia* in May, Nikolai Volkov suggested that all contemporary genres were infected by a willingness to 'cater to the most primitive tastes of the viewers' and, keeping one eye on the box office, to follow rather than to shape those tastes. After finding a number of historical films tainted by this baleful influence, most apparent in their readiness to 'garnish the classics' of Russian literature 'with ambiguous inserts', he noted that this 'pull towards pornography' was also to be found in films on modern life, and, specifically, in *Bed and Sofa*. Its aim to expose the treatment of women as the private property of men was noble; the direction, acting and cinematography were of a high standard; but alas:

> there remains a cold slavering over those combinations of relationships which arise in the situation of a 'wife of two husbands'. It is moreover typical that the authors, having in mind the [popular] demand for something piquant, achieve this piquancy by a constant method of 'oblique hints', or all sorts of symbolic renderings of erotic scenes. The meaning of all the efforts of the authors of *Ménage à trois* can be reduced to the maximum arousal in this plane of the activity of the viewers' fantasy.[30]

Thus, in a discussion that lasted with great intensity over a period of almost five months, the direction, the cinematography, especially the shooting of the Moscow exteriors, and the acting of *Bed and Sofa* all received unstinting and almost universal praise. Those critics who admired the film and who approached it most thoughtfully, such as Khersonsky, were ready to admit that it offered an honest and nuanced assessment of NEP life. Those who attacked it insisted that Soviet people did not live in the way the film portrayed; found its class setting contradictory; were alarmed that the characters were attractive, rather than obvious villains; considered the film pornographic both by virtue of its theme and in the way it addressed it; and were particularly incensed that the authorial stance was not explicitly articulated and that the ending was left open. Yet all these 'defects' were clearly intended by Room, as is apparent from his 1926 statement. He *intended* to say that *meshchanstvo* was not a simple class phenomenon and that Soviet 'good fellows' were capable of extraordinary callousness towards women. Above all, like Lermontov before him, Room *intended* to leave the film open, and to let viewers discuss the issues it raised at length and form their own opinions. 'We have fed people with sweets for long enough.'

It is apparent that much of the dissatisfaction with the film was ideologically motivated, and was part of the battle that was raging at the time over the role of Soviet cinema, and specifically over its contradictory functions as entertainment and as ideology.[31] Room's triumph, in this context, is to have made a formally sophisticated and original film that promoted extremely wide debate, both among critics and among ordinary viewers. Much of that debate was disapproving, particularly among less educated audiences. When the film was shown at a factory cinema in the town of Zlatoust it aroused a storm of protest, and everyone got up and left in disgust.[32] At the first All-Union Party Conference on Cinema, in March 1928, an Irkutsk delegate expostulated: 'You show a film like *Bed and Sofa* in the country, and the peasants come out spitting: "Ah, so that's how they behave in the city." And that's how Sovkino promotes the bond between city and country.'[33]

More sophisticated viewers continued to support the film. Ilia Trainin was both a former chairman of Glavrepertkom, the censorship and repertoire committee, and a member of the board of directors of Sovkino. In his 1928 book *Kino na kul'turnom fronte* [Cinema on the Cultural Front] he insisted that films should continue to reflect the complex nuances of Soviet life in the way that *Bed and Sofa* had done, adding that even communists experienced domestic problems. The extent of the film's fame is apparent from Mayakovsky's poem '"Society's" and "Mine"' ['Obshchee' i 'moe'], published in *Komsomol'skaia pravda* on 5 July 1928. One of a number of poems he wrote at the time excoriating the old *byt*, it attacks the important Soviet official and Party member, 'Ivan Ivanych', 'almost a "leader"', who speaks publicly of women's equality but, when he comes home from work, pulls down the shutters, loosens his waistcoat, and 'here / the hours of private life! / he changes / completely / in Third Meshchanskaia Street manner [po-tret'e-meshchanski]'.

In a further indication of the film's popularity, that same year another leading Futurist poet, Aleksei Kruchenykh, self-published in Moscow a collection called *Govoriashchee kino: 1-ia kniga stikhov o kino: Stsenarii. Kadry. Libretto: Kniga nebyvalaia* [Talking Cinema: First Book of Poems About the Cinema: Screenplays. Sequences. Librettos. An Unprecedented Book]. The collection contained twenty poems on the most popular films and actors (both Soviet and foreign) of the Soviet 1920s, including Buster Keaton and Harold Lloyd. There are two poems inspired by *Bed and Sofa*. The first, 'Liubov' vtroem (Libretto)' [Ménage à trois. A Libretto] relates the full plot of the film from the start (the yardman is likened to Kropotkin) to the tea and jam of the ending. The second, 'Liubov' vtroem (Kadry)' [Ménage à trois. Sequences] revisits the ending of the film and its unresolved questions, suggesting that scriptwriters and directors will continue to find rich material in them.[34]

Room himself summed up with some satisfaction the reactions his film had provoked (and reiterated the stance he had taken in his September 1926 statement about the film) in an article published in the magazine *Zhizn' iskusstva*, 6, 1928:

> People consider that *Bed and Sofa* was the first film of daily life [bytovym fil'mom]. Those who follow the growth and development of our cinema closely will find this to be the first film of daily life not only in the calendar sense.
>
> This film has played an exceptional role in another sphere, which had not yet been touched upon. I am speaking of the matter of enticing the broad masses of viewers into the discussion and analysis of Soviet film.
>
> If you follow the many newspaper reports and assessments of the showings of *Bed and Sofa* that were followed by discussions, it is not difficult to establish that in almost all towns (even very small ones) the release of the film was accompanied by special showings, discussions, questionnaires, collective reviews and so on [...]
>
> I am coming to the most important and significant part of my article, to the phenomenon of the *problem* film, that is to say the kind of film that, besides the normal tasks of capturing daily life (which are difficult enough in themselves), also poses certain problem tasks, touches a certain question of how we construct our daily life. Making a film like this is several times more difficult than making a film that simply portrays day to day life, and in such a case one should not always expect entirely positive results, which satisfy everyone and everything.
>
> Can we demand that a film of daily life, and, moreover, one which poses a problem, addresses a certain important aspect of our day to day experience (the organisation of the new man, the construction of the family, the relations between the sexes) should provide a full and coherent resolution of the problem? After all it's only lazy schoolboys, who don't like doing sums, who start by looking at the answers at the

back of the textbook. Yet it is *precisely this, an answer*, a ready-made solution to the equation, that people expect to get from a problem film.

The true and real task of the problem film of daily life should be, above all, a skillful and lively posing of the question (of course, by means of an interesting and engaging plot). By means of a concrete example the director and the actor must elaborate and reveal the essence of the problem they have posed, must illuminate it and set it out *in such a way* that the viewer sees the task they have set themselves more clearly and understands it better, and, in consequence, that he himself should go on thinking directly about the question raised by the film. Society should discuss and analyse films of this kind with the most acute attention.[35]

Nevertheless, the ideological tide was, by the late 1920s, almost irresistible, and it would wash away the nuanced stance of films like *Bed and Sofa*. Treatment of the love triangle would alter radically (see below) and in 1936 *Bed and Sofa* would be recalled with ideological squeamishness by the critic Boris Alpers as the apogee of the NEP bourgeois comedy and a 'bedroom farce'.[36] In the same year the film was among those banned from exhibition by the State Directorate for the Cinema and Photographic Industry [Gosudarstvennoe upravlenie kinofotopromyshlennosti].[37]

The Fate of the Film in Other Countries at the Time

The film was shown successfully in a number of European countries. In Germany it was known as *Bett und Sofa*, and such was its popularity that, in the words of Winifred Bryher, writing in 1929: 'Eighteen months ago all Germany talked of *Bed and Sofa*. It became tiresome in any cinematic discussion to be silenced with, "But you don't know, you can't judge, you haven't seen *Bed and Sofa*."' It ran in ordinary cinemas in Germany for months.[38] Bryher herself found the failure to go through with the abortion unpersuasive, but, this apart, her praise of the film was lavish:

Up to this moment the film has been magnificent [...] Even with the jar at the end, this must remain one of the great films of the world. It obliterates so many trials, experiments and ifs. There is no further need to talk about what the cinema might do. Here is accomplishment. It gives to the spectator instead of taking from him: a novel sensation to those used to the ordinarily projected films. Room has obtained his effects by using the correct psychological basis for all actions, however minute, and by his capacity to set symbols of the brain processes, in pictures.[39]

The film was also very well received in France, where it bore the title *Trois dans un sous-sol* [Three in a Basement], and was the first Soviet film to be shown uncensored.[40] When Eisenstein took questions after lecturing at the Sorbonne on 17 February 1930 it was the first film (and one of only two) apart from his own that he was asked about. Eisenstein, whose own films of the period were radically different from Room's in both their epic scope and their formal devices, was non-committal: 'It's interesting in terms of the plot. We have a lot of films like that, and they are very necessary because they touch on questions of family ethics and other questions which concern us. It's like a didactic play in which all sorts of moral questions are discussed.'[41]

According to Shklovsky, *Bed and Sofa* also elicited a 'poetic' 'reply' in René Clair's *Sous les toîts de Paris* [Under the Roofs of Paris, 1930], though in fact the links between the films are quite tenuous. In *Sous les toîts de Paris* two friends, Albert and Louis, both fall in love with Pola. At first she seems to respond to Albert's attentions, but when he is imprisoned she realises that her real love is Louis. After his release he acknowledges this, and readily accepts his friend's 'victory'. At the end of the film he is already eyeing up another girl.[42]

The first recorded English response dates from December 1927. The anonymous reviewer for *Close Up* considered it:

a simple story almost crudely told yet astounding in its sheer uncompromise [...] The usual technique is almost ignored, and havoc is made of time sequences by reckless cuts [the copy shown in England was censored, J.G.], by unrelated continuity, by every fault that the amateur can make. And yet here was a film that gripped and had genius. Its very unevenness gave it an odd power; almost, one might say, created a new technique. It should be played without music and its staccato movement would be in accord.[43]

Yet again, the reviewer disliked the scene in the abortion clinic, finding it sentimental and psychologically unpersuasive, since Liuda is too self-centred for motherhood. But 'The amazing quality of the film was that it presented life as it (let us admit it) so often is, and not as most of us try to pretend it should be.'[44] The reviewer concluded that it was 'an historic film', and probably better than Pudovkin's *The Mother*. Readers were recommended to see it 'at all costs', since, 'It is one of the most momentous contributions to film progress yet achieved'.[45]

Those readers wishing to follow Anon's advice were largely thwarted by the fact that the film had not been passed for public exhibition in Britain, even in censored form. But it was shown privately at the Film Society in London on 7 and 8 April 1929, provoking two further notices in *Close Up*. One, by A.W., called it 'a great human document with more truth in it than any dozen of the sex-drenched, sex-debauched films which constitute the great bulk of movie entertainment in Britain today', and pointed out that the same social evils existed in London, Berlin and Paris. A.W. reports an illuminating conversation overheard after the film:

SHE: 'What a disgusting picture!'
HE: 'Yes, darling. If I had know it would be like this I would not have brought you here.'

He ends his review with a regret that 'the Film Society copy was cut, of course' and with the contention that the moral of the film is that 'Woman is the equal of man [...] Woman must be free, independent; the old moral traditions of masculine superiority are wrong. Over-crowding must be abolished [...] A new life, a free life, based on complete social equality', adding, with righteous irony, 'How nasty! How disgusting!'[46] Anon and A.W.'s enthusiasm for the film shines through, despite the problems caused by watching a mutilated print. *Close Up*'s other reviewer, H.C., was considerably less enthusiastic, finding the film 'somewhat of a disappointment', disapproving of the melodramatic elements in the scene in the abortion clinic, and up-braiding the Film Society for their tortured attempts in the programme notes to justify showing a censored copy of the film.[47]

The fullest and most thoughtful Western engagement with Room's film at the time was in Paul Rotha's *The Film Till Now*, first published in London in 1930. For Rotha, while most American films are 'saturated in sex stimulant', and 'every girl chosen for a part in a British film is judged by her amount of sex, according to *outward appearances*', *Bed and Sofa*, whose purpose is to attack 'man's selfish attitude towards women' is 'one of the most sexual pictures ever produced'.[48] Like the Soviet critic Osip Beskin three years earlier, he likened the film to Chaplin's *A Woman of Paris*, though this time the comparison intended the highest praise: 'The joy of watching *A Woman of Paris* unfold its length was only equalled by that of *Bed and Sofa*. With both films the spectator experienced an inward sense of irresistible delight, due, I believe, largely to the design and balance of the continuity.'[49] For Rotha, the strength of Room's direction lay in his narration through the reactions of the characters and through 'small, possibly insignificant, outer actions', a method 'in direct contrast with the methods of the left-wing'. He admired the use of spatial contrast and of gesture, the construction of the situations and the cutting ('so good as to be almost unnoticeable'), all of which contributed to 'an unequalled instance of pure psychological, intimate, cinematic representation of human character'. If it were not for the ending, which Rotha considered a descent into 'sentimental and banal motherhood', and a concession to the policy of discouraging abortion in the USSR, then *Bed and Sofa* 'would have been one of the greatest films yet made'.[50]

For all this praise, *Bed and Sofa* was not shown commercially in England until 1933–34, and then with a number of cuts. It was not allowed commercially in the USA at the time at all.[51] It was, however, shown successfully in a number of other European countries. When, years later, Room went to Lvov (which had by then become part of the Soviet Union) to make his film *Wind from the East* [Veter s vostoka, 1940], a distributor showed him the three-storey house he had built himself on the proceeds of marketing *Bed and Sofa*.[52]

The Subsequent Fate of the Film-makers

Later in 1927, after Room had played the part of a film director in Sergei Komarov's comedy *The Kiss of Mary Pickford* [Potselui Meri Pikford, 1927], Room and Shklovsky again worked together at the Sovkino Moscow studio on *Potholes* [Ukhaby, 1927], a continuation of the themes of the family and parenthood, but this time based on a story by the worker correspondent A. Dmitriev and set in a glass factory. When Tania tells her husband Pavel that she is pregnant, his first reaction, again, is that she should have an abortion. But she has the baby, and when there are cutbacks at the factory, she stays at home to look after it. After the baby's birth, Pavel cools to his wife (he finds nappies a sign of *meshchanstvo*), and takes up with Liza. The factory help the abandoned Tania to get a job in another town. Before leaving she plays the part of an abandoned wife in an amateur theatrical production, which Pavel happens to see. His conscience leads him to leave Liza, who has turned out not to be the woman he imagined. He too decides to start a new life and on the steamer to a new town he meets Tania and they are reconciled. The differences between the resolution of the two films scarcely need to be elaborated, and *Potholes* could even be seen as an act of atonement for the defiance of the earlier film. In *Bed and Sofa* the wife is unemployed, the family is destroyed and the ending is unclear; Soviet morality is considerably better served by *Potholes*, in which the wife, too, is a worker, the husband repents his villainy, and at the film's end the couple embark once more along life's path hand in hand. To quote an intertitle from the film: 'Down with potholes on the path of the new *byt*.'[53]

Despite this, Room's subsequent career was not without difficulties. He experienced particular problems with two later attempts to address the theme of the love triangle. In 1933–34 he worked on *One Summer* [Odnazhdy letom], from a script by the writers Ilf and Petrov, but he was taken off the film when it ran over budget. As eventually completed by the actor Igor Ilinsky and Khanan Shmain in 1936, it is a lame comedy in which two automobile enthusiasts drive their home-made car to Moscow. On the way they both fall in love with the same girl, but if, at the film's end, she does choose between them, her choice is drowned out by a strategically sounding factory whistle. Then in 1936, his brilliant and formally innovative *A Stern Young Man* [Strogii iunosha], based on a script by Iuri Olesha which told the story of the love of member of the Young Communist League for the young wife of an eminent professor, despite resolving the relationship in acceptable Soviet fashion, was banned for 'the coarsest deviations from the style of Socialist Realism'.[54] Room returned to the romantic triangle of husband, wife and young man in one of his last films, *The Garnet Bracelet* [Granatovyi braslet, 1964] taken from a story by Alexander Kuprin. Room died on 26 July 1976.

Room's scriptwriter, Viktor Shklovsky, continued a multi-faceted engagement with the cinema throughout his long career. He wrote theoretical and practical articles and was particularly concerned with the question of the cinematic adaptation of literary classics. He lectured on scriptwriting in the Mezhrabpomfilm Studios in 1929, and his insights, drawn both from his own direct experience and his critical analysis of the work of others, were published as a book in 1931.[55] Among the most notable films drawn from his later scripts were Kuleshov's *Gorizont* [1932] and Pudovkin's *Minin and Pozharsky* [Minin i Pozharskii, 1939], and he continued to script films into the 1970s. He published a major study of Sergei Eisenstein in 1973 and extensive collections of his cinematic writings were published in 1965 and 1985.[56]

The assistant and designer, Sergei Iutkevich, directed his own first full-length film, *Lace* [Kruzheva] in 1928. He went on to become one of the leading Soviet directors, most famous for making several films about Lenin, beginning with *The Man with a Gun* [Chelovek s ruzh'em, 1938].

Both the film's male actors died young. Vladimir Fogel made a number of films in the two years after completing *Bed and Sofa*. He was the unsuccessful lover in Barnet's 1927 lyrical comedy *The Girl with the Hatbox* and a German officer in Pudovkin's *The End of St Petersburg* [Konets Sankt-Peterburga, 1927]. He acted in Fedor Otsep's *Captive Earth* [Zemlia v plenu, 1927], Sergei Komarov's *The Doll with Millions* [Kukla s millionami, 1928] and Grigori Roshal's *The Salamander* [Salamandra, 1928]. But he committed suicide on 8 June 1929 after a long period of depression and nervous illness.

Nikolai Batalov continued to act in films and at the Moscow Arts Theatre. He acted with Fogel again in *Captive Earth*. In the 1930s he played Leva Gorizont in Kuleshov's *Gorizont*, and was one of the *Three Comrades* in Semen Timoshenko's film of that name [Tri tovarishcha, 1935]. But his most important role in that decade was that of Sergeev in Nikolai Ekk's *The Road to Life* [Putevka v zhizn', 1931], the story of the re-education of homeless children in a work colony in the first years after the Revolution. This was the first Soviet sound feature film and, unlike other theatrical actors, Batalov successfully managed to adopt colloquial speech patterns. He was made an 'Honoured Artist of the Republic' in 1933 and given the Order of the Red Banner in 1937. But he had been suffering on and off from tuberculosis since 1923 and, despite being sent for treatment abroad, he died of the disease on 10 November 1937.

Liudmila Semenova worked again for Kozintsev and Trauberg, with small parts in *S.V.D. (The Union of the Great Cause)* [S.V.D. (Soiuz velikogo dela), 1927] and *New Babylon* [Novyi Vavilon, 1929]. Natasha, her character in Fridrikh Ermler's *A Fragment of Empire* [Oblomok imperii, 1929], is once again the wife of two husbands. Her first husband, Filimonov, was concussed during the Civil War, and eleven years after the Revolution he still suffers from amnesia. Meanwhile Natasha has married a 'cultural worker'. Though the film is mainly Filimonov's story, the tale of his recovery of memory and his journey to socialist consciousness, in the treatment of Natasha the film makes several direct references to *Bed and Sofa*. Natasha is first seen at the window of a passing train, though in this case she is not moving off to a life of freedom but in the constraining company of her new husband. When Filimonov begins to remember his past, he comes to Leningrad in search of her. Though the flat which Natasha shares with her husband contains revolutionary journals and the complete works of Lenin, it is also full of bourgeois clutter. While the cultural worker drinks tea and reads the paper, his wife stands meticulously brushing his jacket. When she hands him his hat he angrily tells her that he wants his cap instead. Later the cultural worker is seen addressing a group of factory workers through a loudspeaker: 'Look at your wives ... They are exhausted by the kitchen, by domestic chores.' He admonishes them to seek rather 'a comrade, a friend' in their wives. Yet, like Mayakovsky's 'Ivan Ivanych', this public revolutionary is a tyrant at home. Back in the flat he shouts at Natasha: 'I read lectures about the new *byt*, but my wife is a *meshchanka*, bogged down in her kitchen.' When she serves him soup, he complains that she has not salted it. At the end of the film, Filimonov arrives at the flat and attempts to persuade his wife to leave with him: 'Let's get out of here, Natasha!' Alas, she is too mired in the old *byt* and cannot make the break. As he leaves, Filimonov disgustedly says to the couple, 'Oh, you ... fragments of empire'. The sentence he passes on them echoes Liuda's 'I'm leaving ... I shall never return to your Mesh-chanskaia'. In each film one member of the triangle leaves for ever and enters a new life, while the remaining couple is left in the flat which represents the stultifying thrall of the past. But the class-based distinction between the characters in *A Fragment of Empire* is considerably more conventional than the gender-based resolution of the earlier film.

In the ensuing years Semenova worked more in the theatre than the cinema, though she had small parts in films such as Ivan Pyrev's *At 6 p.m. After the War* [V shest' chasov vechera posle voiny, 1944] and Sergei Gerasimov's *The Young Guard* [Molodaia gvardiia, 1948]. She was memorable as the stern music teacher in Andrei Tarkovsky's debut short *The Steamroller and the Violin* [Katok i skripka, 1960]. She died on 25 May 1990.

The Fate of Room's Themes

The problems of Soviet families continued to be addressed in Soviet films, but now, with society's help, they were resolved. The readiness of the hero of *My Son* [1928] to take on another man's child has been discussed earlier. Two years later, in M. Gall's *I Don't Want a Child* [Ne khochu rebenka, 1930], in which Semenova played the part of a neighbour, the Komsomol brigade shock worker, Olga, becomes pregnant. Work in the factory and her public duties would leave her no time to bring up the child herself, but her husband, Pavel, is utterly opposed to sending the child to a nursery. So Olga decides to have an abortion. Pavel gets the factory collective to dissuade her. With consummately good timing the factory organises a crèche just as Olga is about to give birth. Her husband, repenting of his error, agrees to send the child there. The film's philosophy is best expressed through its subtitle *Isn't Life Fine!* [Razve zhizn' ne prekrasna].

A variation of the theme is provided in Eduard Ioganson's *Life at Full Steam* [Zhizn' na polnyi khod, 1930]. Murkin, a print worker like Volodia in *Bed and Sofa*, marries Natasha, a fellow worker, and they have a son. Natasha finds it hard to combine work and motherhood, but Murkin is categorically against giving the child to a crèche. At first Natasha accepts this, but eventually she leaves her husband, who will not let her take the child. He then gets into the same difficulties as she had, and his work suffers so badly that he gets sacked. So he has to live on his savings and, when they run out, to bring up the child in poverty. Since he is now in the same position as a housewife, he is invited by the house management committee to a meeting of the women who have raised the question of a children's play area. Murkin takes charge of the women's efforts. Natasha, realising his difficulties, starts paying him alimony for their son and, when she realises that his attitudes have changed, she comes back to him.[57]

The reversal of traditional family roles (seen previously in *Katka the Reinette Apple Seller*) finds symbolic expression in Efim Dzigan's *The Woman* [Zhenshchina, 1932], set in a distant village. When a collective farm is set up, a young peasant woman, Masha, decides to become a tractor driver, thus provoking horror and threats from her husband and mockery from her fellow villagers. Not knowing how to combine this work with caring for her small child, she turns to Uliana, an old peasant woman, and together with the chairman of the village Soviet they organise a nursery for the collective farm children. Masha gets work in the tractor repair workshop, where she shows immense courage and proves her right to work as an equal to men.[58]

If men learn the error of their reactionary ways, they can be accepted once more both by their wives and by the collective. If they continue to err, then society, and the film-makers, are merciless. In Igor Savchenko's *A Chance Meeting* [Sluchainaia vstrecha, 1936], the heroine, Irina, another shock worker, this time at the Felix Dzerzhinzky toy factory, meets Grisha, a sports instructor, who has come to the factory to give the workers physical education classes, and who tells her that she will make a champion athlete. He wants to train her for the autumn Spartakiada, the national athletics championships. They marry. When she tells him she is pregnant he is appalled (it is too early, this will ruin everything, maybe when they are forty) and tries to persuade her to have an abortion. Deeply wounded, she leaves him. Petr Ivanych, a fellow worker long in love with Irina, talks to the factory director, who reminds him that 'The Party teaches us to protect the family'. Petr tries to persuade Grisha to ask for Irina's forgiveness ('She's a mother. Do you understand that?'), but to no avail – Grisha leaves.

Three years pass. Irina is bringing up her daughter, with the help of her work collective, and especially of Petr Ivanych, who is ready to take on another man's child. She has returned to her running. At the Spartakiada in Moscow she wins the 400 metres. Grisha, present at the event, tries to get back together with her, but she dismisses him, saying she no longer feels anything for him. Once again, an egotistical man abandons his pregnant wife. But in *A Chance Meeting* disapproval of his behaviour is apparent from the start. He is shown as an unalloyed scoundrel. The setting of the film in a toy factory with resident children 'consultants' and the scenes of happy children which pervade the film only underline the point. At the end of the film Grisha runs from the stadium in lonely disgrace. Irina, Petr Ivanych, and 'their' daughter are united as a model Soviet family, and look out contentedly at the audience, exactly as do Martynov, Marion Dixon and her son at the end of Grigori Alexandrov's musical *The Circus* [Tsirk, 1936].[59]

Grisha, the errant father, is literally written out of the idealised Soviet family, but Irina is fortunate enough to find as a replacement for him a man who has all the qualities that Grisha lacks. As the decade went on, and the theme of Soviet motherhood became more and more ideologised, even those women who were not as fortunate as Irina knew that their children did indeed have a father in Comrade Stalin, the father of all Soviet children, a myth universally fostered, but never as powerfully as in Dziga Vertov's 1937 *Lullaby* [Kolybel′naia], in which mothers from all over the country rejoice at the possibilities given to them by 'great comrade Stalin'. In the words of a contemporary review: 'The fatherly concern of Stalin, who has changed woman, previously oppressed and without rights, into a happy and free participant in the construction of socialism, is shown in every frame of the film.'[60]

Nevertheless, the phenomena of the fatherless child and of the single mother, her husband lost in war, or working in a distant part of the country, or in prison, or generally no good, outlived the Stalinist period and remained ubiquitous, surviving, in cinema as in society, into the post-Soviet years, where a striking example of the fatherless hero is provided by Danila Bagrov, the protagonist of Aleksei Balabanov's highly popular examinations of the hopes and fears of a new generation, *Brother* [Brat, 1997] and *Brother 2* [Brat 2, 2000].[61]

Room's other key theme, of the two male friends who fall in love with the same woman, was made safe in the films of the ensuing decade, channelled into lyricism, innocent humour and the capacity for self-abnegation. In Alexei Popov's *Two Friends, a Model and a Girlfriend* [Dva druga, model' i podruga, 1927], released in January 1928, the friends, Akhov and Makhov, invent the model of the film's title, a machine for making boxes in the soap factory in which they work. They both fall in love with their workmate Dasha. At first the existence of Dasha's fiancé prevents either of them from making any headway, but when finally she throws him over for Makhov, Akhov accepts his defeat with good grace. In Boris Barnet's *By the Bluest of Seas* [U samogo sinego moria, 1935] the two friends are the mechanics Alesha and Iusuf. They both fall in love with Mashenka, a brigade leader at a fishing collective farm on the Caspian Sea. The rivalry is expressed through lyrical comedy, and resolved without conflict when it transpires that Mashenka, too, has a fiancé, a sailor serving in the distant Pacific Ocean. Mashenka remains true to her man, and the friends, aware of the imperatives of duty and fidelity, are happily reconciled in their defeat. The messy emotional realities of *Bed and Sofa* will now be banished from Soviet screens for decades.

If the phenomenon of two male friends falling in love with the same woman could no longer be addressed with the same acuity in the Soviet arts, it continued to preoccupy Western European artists, and was variously examined, and variously resolved by them throughout the century. A striking example, chronologically close to Room but worlds apart in the treatment of the subject, is Noel Coward's relentlessly bright and garrulous *Design for Living* (1933), in which the characters spend their entire time discussing the intricacies of their relationships. Both Otto, an artist, and Leo, a writer, are in love with Gilda, who lives with each of them in turn, in Paris and London. Tiring of their success and self-satisfaction, she leaves them both identical notes and departs to New York to marry dull but dependable Ernest. But his gentle kindness is no substitute for the obsession and vitality she experiences with the abandoned duo, and when they turn up in New York she rushes to be reconciled with them (both), since, in Leo's words, 'We have our own decencies. We have our own ethics. Our lives are a different shape from yours.'[62]

Perhaps the most famous Western cinematic examination of a triangular love affair is François Truffaut's film *Jules and Jim* [Jules et

Jim, 1962]. Here, too, two male friends fall for the same woman, the enigmatic Catherine. Nevertheless, the film differs from *Bed and Sofa* in several fundamental ways. *Jules et Jim* is set in the photogenic past – it begins in 1912 – and makes a calculated frontal attack on the viewer by the deployment of myriad 'charming' details, a stratagem utterly disdained by Room. Though it makes some reference to social history – there are extensive scenes of the First World War – its reading of the relationships is based entirely in the behaviour of the characters, and more specifically in the 'force of nature' that is Catherine. First Catherine marries Jules; then she plans to marry Jim. Both men are so besotted with her that they will accept any eccentricity, any betrayal, since they – and the film – know that she is 'a queen'. Despite brief periods of idyllic country life, Truffaut's characters are not able to sustain their 'pioneering' relationship, but neither can they find the strength to renounce it. There is only one way that the film can end. Catherine takes Jim out in her car and drives them off a bridge to a watery death. Only then can Jules find 'relief'. Though Truffaut's sense of irony is as evident as Room's is, their films have very different agendas; and it is *Jules et Jim* that now seems dated and ingratiating.

Bed and Sofa Rediscovered

For decades Room's film received but cursory ritual mention in Soviet and Western film histories. Jay Leyda, for example, does little more than extend Bryher's synopsis.[63] But in the 1970s, it was taken up by a new generation of critics. In 1971, in the first Western article addressed specifically to the film, Steven P. Hill combined a brief description of it with an overview of Room's career.[64] The following year Beth Sullivan compared its treatment of marital relations with that of Carl Dreyer's *Master of the House* [Du skal ære din Hustru, 1925], in which the nervous breakdown of a wife who has failed to rebel against her oppressive husband finally leads him to change. Though the article devotes more space to Dreyer, Sullivan sees Room's film as socially more progressive.[65] Then in 1974 Molly Haskell described it as 'one of the most extraordinary feminist films of that [the 1920s] or any other time'.[66]

Room's reputation was given an enormous boost by the publication in 1977 of Irina Grashchenkova's book *Abram Room*, which remains to this day the only full-length survey of his career. Its treatment of *Bed and Sofa* combines a detailed description of the filming process, an examination of the characters, an incisive analysis of Room's use of Moscow exteriors and the interior of the flat, and a judicious survey of critical reaction.[67] Another leading Russian critic, Maya Turovskaya, provided an acute and revealing analysis of the role of things in the film in a 'digression' to an article mainly devoted to Lana Gogoberidze's film *Several Interviews on Personal Questions* [Ramdenime interviu pirad sakitkhebze, 1978].[68]

In the 1980s a number of American critics made important contributions to the study of the film. Paul Burns's 1982 article combined a useful explanation of the NEP social context with an acute reading of the film.[69] Denise J. Youngblood first looked at the reception of the film in the context of the battles over the role of Soviet cinema in the late 1920s in her *Soviet Cinema in the Silent Era, 1918–1935* (1985), and expanded the survey in an article of 1989.[70] The same year Judith Mayne included an excellent chapter on the film, alert in particular to the film's sexual politics and to the way imagery is used in it to suggest meaning, in her book on the treatment of women in Soviet silent cinema.[71]

Bed and Sofa Now

The centenary of Room's birth, in 1994, marked by a retrospective of his films at the Cinema Museum in Moscow,[72] drew a new generation of viewers to Room's early work. *Bed and Sofa* spoke particularly eloquently to an epoch whose wild new capitalism was regularly compared to NEP. Moreover, the removal of ideological constraints meant that the culture of the Soviet period could now be analysed with a new freedom. In 1993 Natalia Nusinova considered the film among a number of 1920s and 1930s films that constructed the image of the new Soviet woman, the 'New Eve', and reminded us that Liuda's departure is a 'happy end' which realises 'the eternal dream of the heroes of Russian literature about leaving as a symbol of happiness and the beginning of a new life'.[73] In the same year, Viktor Korotky, in the first of a planned series of articles, examined the role of the exterior scenes, the film's particular use of montage, the relationship of the plot and non-plot material and the role of the actors.[74] Such was the new popularity of the film in Russia that when in 1994 the critic Neya Zorkaya conducted a survey of their favourite silent films among the students of the Higher Courses for Directors and Scriptwriters in Moscow, *Bed and Sofa* finished in first place, well ahead of *The Battleship Potemkin*.[75] In 1996 it gained a wide new audience when it was shown on the Russian NTV television channel in the series *Master Works of Old Cinema* [Shedevry starogo kino] with charmingly stylised music by Taras Buevsky and a sensitive introduction by the critic Naum Kleiman. Since then Zorkaya herself has done much to foster the burgeoning interest in the film, particularly in a wide-ranging 1997 article which places the film in the context of the Russian preoccupation with the 'new man' and the idealised love triangle.[76]

Western critics have turned to the film with increasing frequency. Both Lynne Attwood and Frank Beardow have examined it in the course of their larger surveys of the treatment of women in Soviet cinema,[77] and it has also attracted the attention of critics engaged in broader studies of Russian culture and society.[78]

A further measure of its popularity has been the impulse to re-make it. *Bed and Sofa. A Silent Movie Opera* with libretto by Laurence Klavan and music by Polly Pen, was staged as a workshop production at the Vineyard Theatre in New York in June 1995, and received its world première there on 1 February 1996. As it opens, Volodia is singing:

> The train! The train! The train!
> The birds! The morning! The sun!
> The bridge! The city! The sky!
> Outside! The world!

The script was later published and the performance released on CD.[79]

The plan to make a new version of the film set in contemporary Russia surfaced in the early 1990s. All the scriptwriters who were approached to write *Bed and Sofa – 94* said that it was impossible to give the film a contemporary treatment and that the best thing would be simply to remake it in colour with contemporary actors.[80] The film was eventually made, set in the present, by the director Petr Todorovsky in 1998 as *Ménage à trois* [Retro vtroem]. A comparison of the two films is highly instructive.

The basic plot remains the same. The new film is also set in Moscow. Sergei (played by Sergei Makovetsky) a provincial actor, arrives in Moscow in search of work. He seeks out his old friend and former fellow actor, Kostia (Evgeni Sidikhin). Kostia is now married to Rita (Margarita, played by Elena Iakovleva), who works as a photographer. Since Sergei has nowhere to live, they let him move in with them. Inevitably, Sergei is attracted to Rita. The social setting, too, is comparable with that of *Bed and Sofa*, since the life of Kostia and Rita has all the trappings of the new Russian *meshchanstvo*.

Todorovsky makes liberal use of the devices of the earlier film. He uses intertitles, 'two days passed', 'time flies swiftly', 'winter came', to denote the passage of time. Rita has a number of scenes at the window, and Sergei and Kostia regularly play chess. Other echoes are amusingly modernised. Sergei puts on his Walkman so as not to hear the lovemaking of Kostia and Rita, and on his headphones he listens to English lessons (a fashionable preoccupation of modern Russia), which provide a continuing commentary on the plot through a teaching dialogue concerned with whether men and women can get on. Kostia works on a rooftop on Moscow's Garden Ring, not far from both Third Meshchanskaia Street and the Bolshoi Theatre, and Sergei and Rita, standing with him, get aerial views of Moscow traffic and the cranes on the new building sites. But in an ironic reworking of the 'builder' motif, Sergei's new job is putting up satellite dishes. Indeed, when he comes to check the signal we discover that the TV is showing the scene of Kolia's lunch on the top of the Bolshoi Theatre from *Bed and Sofa*.

Sergei is readier than Kostia to help around the house and do the washing up. When he comes back from a meeting he finds Rita sitting sunlit in a wicker chair, and kisses her. Kostia departs on a ten-day work trip setting up his dishes in a fashionable new development outside Moscow. Sergei tells him he has bought a train ticket to leave Moscow, since 'I am very fond of your wife'. Kostia refuses to take this seriously and tears up the ticket. So Sergei and Rita are thrown together.

Kostia comes back, bearing a bucket of red whortleberries, and plays a little joke on his wife. Sergei tells him what has been going on, but Rita insists 'Sergei, stay!' ('Sergei, ostan´sia'; compare Liuda's, 'Volodia, ostanetsia' in *Bed and Sofa*), so Kostia leaves. Kostia later returns to the flat and Rita shows tenderness towards him. In a subtle modernisation of the fortune-telling of the earlier film Rita cuts up photographs she has taken of the two men and tries to turn them into a composite 'husband'.

All three are now together, and for a while everything goes well. But, on a river-boat trip, Rita announces that she is pregnant. Initially the men express delight, but when she tells them that she does not know who the father is they both agree that she should have an abortion. 'It's my child', replies Rita, and, calling them 'nonentities' [nichtozhestva], she throws herself into the river. The film ends in winter, at what is styled a posthumous exhibition of her paintings ... but suddenly the door bell rings and a baby is heard crying outside.

The characters' names in *Ménage à trois* are not those of *Bed and Sofa*; nor are they those of Todorovsky's actors. Instead he gives them bird surnames, making a charming reference to another NEP love triangle, Barnet's *The Girl with the Hatbox*. In that film the heroine, played by Anna Sten, was Natasha Korosteleva [Corncrake]; her boyfriend was Ilia Snegirev [Bullfinch]; while her unsuccessful suitor, the railway cashier played by Vladimir Fogel, was named Fogelev [Bird] in an allusion to the actor's own name. In *Ménage à trois* the surname of Kostia and Rita is Skvortsov [Starling] and that of Sergei Kukushkin [Cuckoo, a shameless signposting of his later behaviour]. Todorovsky also makes other allusions to early cinema, with long 'silent' episodes and a running preoccupation with Chaplin.

At the same time the film is explicitly of its own era. People eat Big Macs and bananas, and Kostia goes off on his work trip to earn the money for a better car. The plot is opened out not just into all of Moscow – this heroine is certainly not confined to her flat – but also into the whole country, with a prologue episode set in an unspecified Caucasian war.

Ménage à trois is attractively performed by its three star actors, but its relationship to *Bed and Sofa* is an uneasy one. Though male chauvinism is clearly as prevalent now as it was in the 1920s, most of the social and political factors that sited the earlier film so securely in its period are no longer relevant. The addition of several new characters, including a wife for Sergei, doubling and tripling the plot, perversely universalises the story and distorts the link to the original source. The sentimental ending negates the openness of the earlier film. But the film's major miscalculation is to stake so much on 'charm', something hinted at by the meaningless Russian title 'Retro vtroem' (literally 'Retro in three', a play on Room's title 'Liubov' vtroem', 'Love in Three'); in fact the film has absolutely no historical sense, and all its 'retro' elements – the design of the intertitles, the period clothes the characters dress up in, the arrangements of 1930s music, Rita's 'turn' as Marilyn Monroe – are superficial and unfocused. In the end, *Ménage à trois* is toothless and unsatisfying, lacking the authenticity and power to move of its alleged model.[81]

Todorovsky's compromises provide valuable clues to the nature of Room's achievements. *Bed and Sofa* is clear-sighted both about the contradictions of the epoch in which it is set and about the behaviour of its characters. It neither idealises nor sentimentalises. It does not offer pat solutions, either social or behavioural, for intractable problems. It is shot with exemplary tightness and rigour and acted with breathtaking naturalness and energy. It shows that a film story that eschews dramatic events for the fine patterning of ordinary life can also be compulsively engaging. More than seventy years after it was made it speaks to new viewers both about the Soviet past and about their own present. It helps us understand why the Soviet experiment to create the new man and the new woman was doomed to failure. It also tells us just how much of human experience is unchanging.

Notes

1. There is a bibliography of reviews in R. Sheldon (ed.), *Viktor Shklovsky. An International Bibliography of Works By and About Him* (Ann Arbor, MI, 1977), pp. 113–15. There is a helpful selection of the contemporary responses to the film in '"Tret'ia Meshchanskaia": otkliki pressy', published by R. Iangirov, *Iskusstvo kino*, 3, 1998, pp. 15–17. There are also very useful analyses of the press reaction, and extracts from it, in D. Youngblood, 'The Fiction Film as a Source for Soviet Social History: the *Third Meshchanskaia Street* Affair', *Film and History*, 19, 3, 1989, pp. 50–60; and D. Youngblood, *Soviet Cinema in the Silent Era, 1918–1935* [1985] (Austin, TX, 1991), pp. 119–22. I have not always been able to establish the exact dates of reviews, but have tried, judging by the issue numbers, to provide a chronological analysis of responses here.

2. K. Ganzenko, 'Sovetskii byt na sovetskom ekrane', *Kinofront*, 1, 1927, pp. 9–12, quoted in Youngblood, 'The Fiction Film as a Source', p. 55; and *Nikolai Petrovich Batalov. Stat'i, vospominaniia, pis'ma* (Moscow, 1971), p. 199.

3. V. Pertsov, 'Zametki o sovetskoi bytovoi kartine', *Sovetskoe kino*, 1, 1927, quoted in *Istoriia sovetskogo kino*, Vol. 1 (Moscow, 1969), p. 388; and '"Tret'ia Meshchanskaia": otkliki pressy', p. 16.

4. The date of the meeting is taken from Youngblood, 'The Fiction Film as a Source', p. 55. The resolution was published as '"Tret'ia Meshchanskaia". Rezoliutsiia ARK', *Kinofront*, 4, 1927, p. 21. Though Denise J. Youngblood suggests that this issue of the journal appeared in March (Youngblood, 'The Fiction Film as a Source', p. 55), a calculation based on the fact that *Kinofront* was at the time a fortnightly publication (Youngblood, *Soviet Cinema in the Silent Era*, p. 272, note 57) would place it in the second half of February. The resolution is quoted from Grashchenkova, *Abram Room* (Moscow, 1977), p. 110. See also Youngblood, *Soviet Cinema in the Silent Era*, pp. 119–20; V. Korotkii, '"Tret'ia Meshchanskaia" Abrama Rooma: nekotorye nachala analiza fil'ma stat'ia 1', *Tiana-Tolkai*, 1, 1993, p. 50.

5. P. A. Bliakhin, 'Tret'ia Meshchanskaia', *Kino*, 4, 22 January 1927; quoted in Grashchenkova, *Abram Room*, p. 111; Youngblood, *Soviet Cinema in the Silent Era*, p. 272, note 60.

6. G. Giber, 'Kak snimalas' "Tret'ia Meshchanskaia"', *Sovetskii ekran*, 5, 29 January 1927, p. 4.

7. K. Denisov, 'Meshchanstvo v kino', *Sovetskii ekran*, 5, 29 January 1927, p. 3; quoted in '"Tret'ia Meshchanskaia": otkliki pressy', p. 15.

8. N. Iakovlev, 'Pervosortnaia meshchanskaia. (Diskussionno)', *Kino*, 5, 29 January 1927, p. 3; quoted in Nusinova, 'Novaia Eva', *Iskusstvo kino*, 6, 1993, p. 131; Youngblood, *Soviet Cinema in the Silent Era*, p. 120.

9. Kh. Khersonskii, 'Rasskaz o meshchanstve. (Diskussionno)', *Kino*, 5, 29 January 1927, p. 4. In her analysis of the film's reception in *Soviet Cinema in the Silent Era*, p. 120, Denise J. Youngblood describes the negative reviews by Denisov, in *Sovetskii ekran* and Iakovlev, in *Kino*, as 'two perfectly coordinated denunciations of the film', and notes that Iakovlev was the editor of *Sovetskii ekran*; she makes the same point in 'The Fiction Film as a Source', p. 55. But it is important to note that both journals also carried positive pieces in the same issues. Youngblood also refers to the film as 'under siege' and to ARK as its 'lone defender' ('The Fiction Film as a Source', p. 55). In support of this argument she juxtaposes critical reviews written several weeks apart. While it is certainly the case that the film elicited a number of scathing reviews, many of them connected with a more general campaign against the policies of Sovkino, at whose Moscow studio *Bed and Sofa* had been made, and against ARK, with which Room was closely associated, as Youngblood has shown in *Soviet Cinema in the Silent Era*, pp. 109–32, it should be stressed that it also continued to elicit considerable praise from a number of sources, as will be seen from the wide range of opinion expressed in later reviews.

10. *Sovetskii ekran*, 6, 5 February 1927.

11. O. Beskin, 'Neigrovaia fil'ma', *Sovetskoe kino*, 7, 1927, pp. 9–11; quoted in Youngblood, *Soviet Cinema in the Silent Era*, p. 114; Youngblood, 'The Fiction Film as a Source', pp. 55, 57. *A Woman of Paris* was directed by Charles Chaplin in 1923.

12. Argo, poem in *Sovetskii ekran*, 10, 1927; reprinted in '"Tret'ia Meshchanskaia": otkliki pressy', p. 15.

13. 'Kazhetsia, podletsy', *Leningradskaia pravda*, 8 March 1927; quoted in M. Dolinskii and S. Chertok (eds), *Ekran 1968–1969* (Moscow, 1969), p. 24.

14. Sha, 'ARK o "Tret'ei Meshchanskoi"', *Novyi zritel'*, 11, 1927, p. 13. For the attack on ARK, see note 9 above.

15. 'O linii ARK. Pis'mo v redaktsiiu', *Kino*, 13, 29 March 1927, p. 2; quoted in Grashchenkova *Abram Room*, p. 111; Youngblood, *Soviet Cinema in the Silent Era*, p. 121.

16. Grashchenkova, *Abram Room*, p. 85; D. Youngblood, *Movies for the Masses. Popular Cinema and Soviet Society in the 1920s* (Cambridge, 1992), p. 161.

17. M. Bystritsky, review in *Sovetskii ekran*, 12, 1927; quoted in '"Tret'ia Meshchanskaia": otkliki pressy', pp. 15–16.

18. Valerin, review in *Nasha gazeta*, 20 March 1927; quoted in 'Tretia Mechtchanskaia / Trois dans un soul-sol ou L'amour à trois', *Le Film muet soviétique* (Brussels, 1965), pp. 32–3.

19. A. Zuev, '"Liubov' vtroem"', *Pravda*, 22 March 1927, p. 6.

20. On the foundation of ODSK see R. Taylor and I. Christie (eds), *The Film Factory: Russian and Soviet Cinema in Documents 1896–1939* (London, 1988), pp. 134–5; on ARK's role, see ibid., p. 103. When ODSK was founded, ARK became an autonomous section of it.

21. Report in *Kino*, 12, 22 March 1927, pp. 4–5; quoted in '"Tret'ia Meshchanskaia": otkliki pressy', pp. 16–17.

22. M. Bleiman, review in *Leningradskaia pravda*, 23 March 1927; quoted from Grashchenkova, *Abram Room*, p. 109; date taken from Sheldon (ed.), *Viktor Shklovsky. An International Bibliography*, p. 114.

23. The word 'sumbur', muddle, as a term of artistic abuse would become notorious on 28 January 1936 in the title of a *Pravda* attack, 'Sumbur vmesto muzyki' [Muddle instead of music], on Shostakovich's opera *A Lady Macbeth of the Mtsensk District*

24. V.S., 'Krasnoarmeitsy o fil'me "Liubov' vtroem"', *Pravda*, 23 March 1927, p. 6.

25. N.V., review in *Trud*, 24 March 1927; quoted in 'Tretia Mechtchanskaia / Trois dans un soul-sol ou L'amour à trois', p. 32.

26. N. Chuzhak, 'Slezlivaia komediia', *Zhizn' iskusstva*, 13, 1927, pp. 5–6.

27. L. Vul'fov, 'Liubov' vtroem', *Kino*, 13, 29 March 1927, p. 4; quoted in Korotkii, '"Tret'ia Meshchanskaia" Abrama Rooma', p. 60, note 19.

28. Youngblood makes the claim in 'The Fiction Film as a Source', p. 56.

She returns to the question (and draws attention to the anomaly) in *Movies for the Masses*, p. 161 and note 49, pp. 216–17, from where the information about the film's popularity is taken.

29. O. Brik, 'Polpobedy', *Kino*, 15, 12 April 1927, p. 3.

30. N. Volkov, 'Omeshchanivanie sovetskoi fil'my', *Izvestiia*, 106, 12 May 1927, p. 4.

31. There is an excellent discussion of this in Youngblood, *Movies for the Masses*, especially pp. 35–49.

32. Report in *Kino*; quoted in Grashchenkova, *Abram Room*, p. 109.

33. Report in B. Ol'khovyi (ed.), *Puti kino* (Moscow, 1929); quoted in J. Leyda,*Kino. A History of the Russian and Soviet Cinema* (London, 1973), p. 245. The bond [smychka] between city and country was a major plank of political propaganda at the time.

34. I. Trainin, *Kino na kul'turnom fronte* (Leningrad, 1928); quoted in Youngblood, *Soviet Cinema in the Silent Era*, pp. 128–9; Maiakovskii, *PSS*, Vol. 9, pp. 152–6 (p. 153); A. Kruchenykh, *Stikhotvoreniia. Poemy. Romany. Opera* (St Petersburg, 2001), pp. 196–201.

35. Quoted in E. S. Gromov and others (eds), *Sovetskie kino-rezhissery o kino. Partiinost'. Narodnost'. Sotsialisticheskii realizm* (Moscow, 1986), pp. 125–6.

36. B. Al'pers, article in *Kino*, 21 March 1936; quoted in '"Tret'ia Meshchanskaia": otkliki pressy', p. 17.

37. The State Directorate published a list of unsuitable films each year. See *Repertuarnyi ukazatel'* (Moscow, 1936); quoted in P. Kenez, *Cinema and Soviet Society, 1917–1953* (Cambridge, 1992), pp. 144, 155.

38. W. Bryher, *Film Problems of Soviet Russia* (Territet, Switzerland, 1929), pp. 72, 75.

39. Ibid., pp. 74, 75.

40. Burns, 'An NEP Moscow Address: Abram Room's The Meshchanskiaia (Bed and Sofa) in Historical Context', *Film and History*, 12, 4, 1982, p. 81, note 2.

41. S. Eizenshtein, 'Printsipy novogo russkogo fil'ma. Doklad S. M. Eizenshteina v sorbonnskom universitete', *Izbrannye proizvedeniia v shesti tomakh* (Moscow, 1964–71), Vol. 1, pp. 547–59 (p. 556). English translation, as 'The Principles of the New Russian Cinema', in S. Eisenstein, *Selected Works. Vol. 1: Writings, 1922–34*, ed. and trans. Richard Taylor (London and Bloomington, IN, 1988), pp. 195–202.

42. V. Shklovskii, 'Tret'ia Meshchanskaia' [1963], in his *Za sorok let* (Moscow, 1965), pp. 104–7 (p. 106). On *Sous les toîts de Paris*, see R. C. Dale, *The Films of René Clair* (Metuchen, NJ and London, 1986), Vol. 1, pp. 139–59, Vol. 2, pp. 97–112. There is a detailed synopsis in Vol. 2, pp. 97–111. Neither in Dale's analysis, nor in the contemporary reviews he quotes, is there any mention of *Bed and Sofa*.

43. Anon, 'Bed and Sofa', *Close Up*, December 1927, pp. 69–74 (p. 69).

44. Ibid., p. 73.

45. Ibid., p. 74.

46. A.W., 'Bed and Sofa at the Film Society', Close Up, May 1929, pp. 58–60.

47. H.C., 'Note on Bed and Sofa', Close Up, May 1929, pp. 61–2. The programme notes were by Ivor Montagu, and revealed that even after the removal of any reference to abortion the British Board of Film Censors was not prepared to certify the film for public exhibition. See G. Turvey, '"That insatiable body". Ivor Montagu's Confrontation with British Film Censorship', Journal of Popular British Cinema, 3, 2000, pp. 31–44 (pp. 33–4). On Montagu's enthusiasm for the film, see Grashchenkova, Abram Room, p. 96.

48. P. Rotha, The Film Till Now [1930] (London, 1967), p. 144.

49. Ibid., p. 169.

50. Ibid., pp. 240–1.

51. S. P. Hill, 'Bed and Sofa (Tretia Meshchanskaia)', Film Heritage, 7, 1, 1971, pp. 17–20 (p. 17).

52. Grashchenkova, Abram Room, p. 125.

53. Potholes has been lost, but the synopsis is taken from the entry on the film in Sovetskie khudozhestvennye fil'my. Annotirovannyi katalog, Vol. 1 (Moscow, 1961), p. 132, and from a version of the script, A. Room, V. Shklovskii, 'Ukhaby', Iz istorii kino, 9, 1974, pp. 96–122, with an introduction by I. Grashchenkova, 'Vospitanie chuvstv', ibid., pp. 86–95.

54. E. Margolit and V. Shmyrov (eds), (Iz'iatoe kino) Katalog sovetskikh igrovykh kartin, ne vypushchennykh vo vsesoiuznyi prokat po zavershenii v proizvodstve ili iz''iatikh iz deistvuiushchego fil'mofonda v god vypuska na ekran (1924–1953) (Moscow, 1995), p. 55. For an exhaustive analysis of the fate of A Strict Youth, and an overview of Room's career, see M. Michalsky, Iurii Olesha, Abram Room and Strogii iunosha – Artistic Form and Political Context, unpublished PhD thesis, School of Slavonic and East European Studies, University of London, 1999.

55. V. Shklovskii, Kak pisat' stsenarii (Moscow and Leningrad, 1931).

56. V. Shklovskii, Eizenshtein [1973] (Moscow, 1978); Za sorok let (Moscow, 1965); Za 60 let. Raboty o kino (Moscow, 1985).

57. Both I Don't Want a Child and Life at Full Steam are now lost. Plot details are taken from Sovetskie khudozhestvennye fil'my. Annotirovannyi katalog, Vol. 1, pp. 385–6, and 371–2.

58. On I Don't Want a Child and The Woman see Nusinova, 'Novaia Eva', pp. 133–4.

59. It is important to note that the version of A Chance Meeting which was finally released is very different from the film first made by Savchenko, which was, in the words of Evgenii Margolit, 'simply destroyed, the film came out in a heavily altered version'. E. Margolit, 'Perechityvaia istoriiu sovetskogo kino', in A. S. Troshin (ed.), Close-up. Istoriko-teoreticheskii seminar vo VGIKe (Moscow, 1999), pp. 188–210 (p. 198).

60. S. Aleksandrov, review in Kino, 17 November 1937; quoted in A. Dem-

enok (ed.), *Kino totalitarnoi epokhi* (Moscow, 1989), p. 15. On *Lullaby* see also Nusinova, 'Novaia Eva', p. 134.

61. A striking example of the genre is Viacheslav Krishtofovich's *Adam's Rib* [Rebro Adama, 1990] in which three generations of women live in the same flat and await the arrival of a fourth. There is a good discussion of the issues raised here in E. Margolit, 'Starye novye amazonki, ili Zdravstvuite, babushka!', *Iskusstvo kino*, 6, 1991, pp. 42–6.

62. N. Coward, *Design for Living* (London, 1972), p. 127.

63. Leyda, *Kino*, pp. 214–16.

64. Hill, 'Bed and Sofa (Tretia Meshchanskaia)'.

65. B. Sullivan, 'Bed and Sofa / Master of the House', *Women and Film*, 1, 1972, pp. 21–5.

66. M. Haskell, *From Reverence to Rape* [1974] (Chicago, 1987), pp. 320–1. Haskell's reading of the scene in the abortion clinic has been discussed above.

67. Grashchenkova, *Abram Room*, pp. 84–114. Grashchenkova's pioneering work has been widely acknowledged earlier in this study.

68. Turovskaia, '"Zhenskii fil'm" – chto eto takoe?' [1981], in her *Pamati tekushchego mgnoveniia* (Moscow, 1987), pp. 251–3.

69. Burns, 'An NEP Moscow address'.

70. Youngblood, *Soviet Cinema in the Silent Era*, pp. 119–22; Youngblood, 'The Fiction Film as a Source for Soviet Social History'. Youngblood returns briefly to the film in her *Movies for the Masses*, pp. 160–1. The very useful material presented by Youngblood has been widely acknowledged earlier in this study.

71. J. Mayne, '*Bed and Sofa* and the Edge of Domesticity', in her *Kino and the Woman Question. Feminism and Soviet Silent Film* (Columbus, OH, 1989), pp. 110–29. The achievement of Mayne's insightful article has been widely acknowledged earlier in this study.

72. On this see V. Zabrodin (ed.), *Abram Matveevich Room. 1894–1976. Materialy k retrospektive fil'mov* (Moscow, 1994).

73. Nusinova, 'Novaia Eva', pp. 130–2 (p. 132).

74. Korotkii, '"Tret'ia Meshchanskaia" Abrama Rooma'.

75. N. Zorkaia, 'K 100–letiiu Abrama Rooma. "Kruglyi stol" v Muzee kino', *Kinovedcheskie zapiski*, 24, 1994–95, p. 167.

76. N. Zorkaia, 'Brak vtroem – sovetskaia versiia', *Iskusstvo kino*, 5, 1997, pp. 89–97; much of this material was repeated in more provocative form in her 1999 study 'Gendernye problemy v sovetskom kino 30-kh godov', which has been referred to earlier in this study.

77. L. Attwood, 'Women, Cinema and Society', in L. Attwood (ed.), *Red Women on the Silver Screen. Soviet Women and Cinema from the Beginning to the End of the Communist Era* (London, 1993), pp. 17–132 (on *Bed and Sofa*, pp. 46–8); F. Beardow, 'Soviet Cinema: Women – Icons or

Individuals? – Part 1', *Rusistika*, 9, 1994, pp. 22–42 (on *Bed and Sofa*, pp. 31–4).

78. See S. Boym, *Common Places. Mythologies of Everyday Life in Russia* (Cambridge, MA, and London, 1994), pp. 133–4; O. Matich, 'Remaking the Bed: Utopia in Daily Life', in J. Bowlt and O. Matich (eds), *Laboratory of Dreams. The Russian Avant-garde and Cultural Experiment* (Stanford, CA, 1996), pp. 75–6; E. Naiman, *Sex in Public. The Incarnation of Early Soviet Ideology* (Princeton, NJ, 1997), pp. 202–3; F. Wigzell, *Reading Russian Fortunes. Print Culture, Gender and Divination in Russia from 1765* (Cambridge, 1998), pp. 172–3.

79. *Bed and Sofa. A Silent Movie Opera*, libretto by Laurence Klavan, music by Polly Pen, Dramatists Play Service Inc. (New York, 1997). In the original production, directed by Andre Ernotte, the cast was Terri Klausner as Ludmilla, Michael X. Martin as Kolya and Jason Workman as Volodya. The CD is published by Varèse Sarabande Records, Inc, 1996, VSD-5729.

80. 'K 100-letiiu Abrama Rooma. "Kruglyi stol" v Muzee kino', p. 167.

81. The critic Natal'ia Sirivlia has called it a 'sugary imitation of family *byt* and love relations'. 'Vtorye stanut pervymi', *Iskusstvo kino*, 8, 1998, pp. 68–74 (p. 73).

Further Reading

On the Film

In English

Burns, P. E., 'An NEP Moscow Address: Abram Room's *Third Meshchanskaia (Bed and Sofa)* in historical context', *Film and History*, 12, 4, 1982, pp. 73–81.

Hill, S. P., 'Bed and Sofa (Tretia Meshchanskaia)', *Film Heritage*, 7, 1, 1971, pp. 17–20.

Mayne, J., '*Bed and Sofa* and the Edge of Domesticity', in her *Kino and the Woman Question. Feminism and Soviet Silent Film* (Columbus, OH, 1989), pp. 110–29.

Sullivan, B., 'Bed and Sofa / Master of the House', *Women and Film*, 1972, 1, pp. 21–5.

Youngblood, D. J., 'The Fiction Film as a Source for Soviet Social History: the *Third Meshchanskaia Street* Affair', *Film and History*, 19, 3, 1989, pp. 50–60.

In Russian

Grashchenkova, I., *Abram Room* (Moscow, 1977), pp. 84–114.

Korotkii, V., '"Tret´ia Meshchanskaia" Abrama Rooma: nekotorye nachala analiza fil´ma. Stat´ia 1', *Tiani-Tolkai*, 1, 1993, pp. 33–60.

Zorkaia, N., 'Brak vtroem – sovetskaia versiia', *Iskusstvo kino*, 5, 1997, pp. 89–97.

— 'Gendernye problemy v sovetskom kino 30-kh godov. "Liubovnyi treugol´nik" kak kul´turologicheskaia i sotsiologicheskaia problema. (Kommentarii k "Tret´ei Meshchanskoi" A. Rooma)', *Close-Up. Istoriko-teoreticheskii seminar vo VGIKe*, ed. A. S. Troshin (Moscow, 1999), pp. 210–19.

Social and Cultural Background

Benjamin, W., 'Moscow' [1927], in his *One-Way Street and Other Writings* (London, 1979), pp. 177–208.

— *Moscow Diary* (London, 1986).

Brodsky Farnsworth, B., 'Bolshevik Alternatives and the Soviet Family: the 1926 Marriage Law Debate', in D. Atkinson, A. Dallin and G. Warshofsky Lapidus (eds), *Women in Russia* (Stanford, CA, 1977; Hassocks, 1978), pp. 139–65.

Buchli, V., *An Archaeology of Socialism* (Oxford and New York, 1999).

Evans Clements, B., 'The Birth of the New Soviet Woman', in A. Gleason, P. Kenez and R. Stites (eds), *Bolshevik Culture: Experiment and Order in the Russian Revolution* (Bloomington, IN, 1985), pp. 220–37.

— 'The Utopianism of the Zhenotdel', *Slavic Review*, 51, 3, 1992, pp. 485–96.

Goldman, W. Z., 'Women, Abortion and the State, 1917–1936', in B. Evans Clements, B. Alpern Engel and C. D. Worobec (eds), *Russia's Women: Accommodation, Resistance, Transformation* (Berkeley, CA, 1991), pp. 243–66.

— *Women, the State and Revolution. Soviet Family Policy and Social Life, 1917–1936* (Cambridge, 1993).

Johnson, R. E., 'Family Life in Moscow during NEP', in S. Fitzpatrick, A. Rabinowitch and R. Stites (eds), *Russia in the Era of NEP. Explorations in Soviet Society and Culture* (Bloomington and Indianapolis, IN, 1991), pp. 106–24.

Matich, O., 'Remaking the Bed: Utopia in Daily Life', in J. Bowlt and O. Matich (eds), *Laboratory of Dreams. The Russian Avant-Garde and Cultural Experiment* (Stanford, CA, 1996), pp. 59–78.

Naiman, E., *Sex in Public. The Incarnation of Early Soviet Ideology* (Princeton, NJ, 1997).

Rosenberg, W. G. (ed.), *Bolshevik Visions: First Phase of the Cultural Revolution in Soviet Russia* [1984] 2nd edn (Ann Arbor, MI, 1990), Part 1, *The Culture of a New Society: Ethics, Gender, the Family, Law and Problems of Tradition*.

Stites, R. *The Women's Liberation Movement in Russia. Feminism, Nihilism and Bolshevism 1860–1930* (Princeton, NJ, 1978, 1991).